HERMANN KELLER

≫≫ ≫≫ ≫≫ ≪≪ ≪≪ ≪≪

Phrasing and Articulation

≫≫ ≫≫ ≫≫ ≪≪ ≪≪ ≪≪

A Contribution to a Rhetoric of Music

With 152 Musical Examples

Translated by

LEIGH GERDINE

New York

The Norton Library

W · W · Norton & Company · Inc ·

COPYRIGHT © 1973, 1965 BY W. W. NORTON & COMPANY, INC.

First published in the Norton Library 1973

W. W. Norton & Company, Inc. is the publisher of current
or forthcoming books on music by Putnam Aldrich, William Austin,
Anthony Baines, Philip Bate, Sol Berkowitz, Friedrich Blume, How-
ard Boatwright, Nadia Boulanger, Paul Brainerd, Nathan Broder,
Manfred Bukofzer, John Castellini, John Clough, Doda Conrad,
Aaron Copland, Hans David, Paul Des Marais, Otto Erich Deutsch,
Frederick Dorian, Alfred Einstein, Gabriel Fontrier, Harold Gleason,
Richard Franko Goldman, Noah Greenberg, Donald Jay Grout,
James Haar, F. L. Harrison, Daniel Heartz, Richard Hoppin, John
Horton, Edgar Hunt, A. J. B. Hutchings, Charles Ives, Roger
Kamien, Hermann Keller, Leo Kraft, Stanley Krebs, Paul Henry
Lang, Lyndesay G. Langwill, Jens Peter Larsen, Jan LaRue, Maurice
Lieberman, Irving Lowens, Joseph Machlis, Carol McClintock,
Alfred Mann, W. T. Marrocco, Arthur Mendel, William J. Mitchell,
Douglas Moore, Joel Newman, John F. Ohl, Carl Parrish, Vincent
Persichetti, Marc Pincherle, Walter Piston, Gustave Reese, Alexander
Ringer, Curt Sachs, Denis Stevens, Robert Stevenson, Oliver Strunk,
Francis Toye, Bruno Walter, J. T. Westrup, Emanuel Winternitz,
Walter Wiora, and Percy Young.

Library of Congress Cataloging in Publication Data
Keller, Hermann, 1885–
   Phrasing and articulation.
   (The Norton library)
   Translation of Phrasierung und Artikulation.
   Bibliography: p.
   1. Music—Interpretation (Phrasing, dynamics, etc.)
I. Title.
[MT75.K443 1973]   781.6'3   72-13069
ISBN 0-393-00681-6

Translator's Preface to the Norton Library Edition

≫≫ ≫≫ ≫≫ ≪≪ ≪≪ ≫≫

This little book is a very important book. Because my own contribution to it is minimal, I can call its value to attention without being offensive. It does require close, careful reading; it does require frequent reference to the music it discusses; it does presume familiarity with much music literature and competence in music history. For example, there is here no general explanation of the fact that the pattern of the dotted eighth and sixteenth notes together in the Baroque (pages 38-39 and 79) is to be interpreted in at least three different rhythmic values, according to context: a) in a triplet context, it becomes the equivalent of a quarter and an eighth note together in a triplet slur; b) in the French overture style, the dotted eighth is given only part of its value, a substantial rest is interpolated, and the value of the sixteenth note is greatly shortened (sometimes merely halved); and c) it sometimes means exactly what it stands for in the twentieth century.

For a number of years, it had been my intention to write a book such as this. It was, therefore, a gratifying surprise to me to stumble on one already written in German, and done much better than I could have done it. Over several years, I then managed both to get this volume translated and to stimulate the translation and publication of other works of Hermann Keller, to make them available to the English speaking student.

In my own teaching, I had been much concerned with what I termed "articulatory sub-patterns" in the music of Bach. In part, Keller covers this in "The Construction of Groups through Articulation" (Chapter Six); but my term may suggest other useful insights. I have some disagreement with details in Keller. That isn't particularly important. For example, however, I find that I prefer my own articulations for some fugue subjects in *The Well-Tempered Clavier* to his. But I approach that work from the point of view of a pianist; he was looking at it perhaps more as an organist. As Keller points out (page 4), "there is . . . as a rule only one possible, thoughtful phrasing, but there are several possibilities of articulation." Keller's suggestions (pages 86-88) are very thoughtful and stylistically correct if, to me, somewhat conservative because the piano allows for greater sensitivity of articulatory refinement (Keller might well have disagreed). As a case in point, I might cite the b flat minor fugue in Book I: on the piano, I can only make the stretto (measure 67 and following) clear where all five voices enter one after another *if* the two half notes of the subject are detached slightly, not (as Keller suggests) "heavily portamentoed;" then the cascading stretto works, and the half notes with double meanings can be heard with both meanings. But from reading Keller the student will have a scholarly point of reference from which he can add his own improvements when his knowledge is sufficient.

It is perhaps regrettable that Keller here neglects the articulation of the preludes, which are sometimes of greater musical significance than the fugues appended to them. He does deal with both preludes and fugues in his *Das Wohltemperierte Klavier von J. S. Bach* (which I have also translated, but which has not yet found a publisher).

The serious music student will find here a competent discussion of one of the most important areas of music, articulation, an area astonishingly neglected both in the literature and in curricula. Perhaps only a half dozen of the finest musicians alive have fully grasped its critical contribution. In distinguished performances, articulation is that element which transfigures music, once the rudiments can be assumed. Professor Clapp at the University of Iowa used to suggest to his piano students that they practice their scales and arpeggios with at least five distinct dynamic gradations, which they could then produce on demand. He insisted that, from this as a base, the intermediate gradations could also be produced with ease. In my own teaching, I have asked students (more importantly, I think) to practice their scales and arpeggios in varying articulatory patterns, both in order to be able to produce specific articulatory requirements easily on demand and to sensitize them to the rich potential of fine articulatory discrimination. There remain the problems of variants, intermediate gradations, and combinations as further challenges.

The graduate student seeking an important, undiscovered area of music for research—something to be more than a filling-in of a gap with a study of a composer sufficiently unimportant yet to have been exhumed —might well look carefully at some of Keller's suggestions. He lists (pages 11-12) significant areas for real musical research; he says

obliquely (page 9) some things about aesthetic theory and the relationship of music and words; and he is kinder to organists (page 89) than I
have been when he points out very gently that accent on the organ can
only be created through articulation. I observe that most organists have
now mastered the idea that one can play legato *or* staccato; few of them
make much of the possible variants, gradations, and combinations which
lie between. Virtually none of them understand that accent on the organ
is to be created through articulation.

Now that this valuable little book is to appear in paperback, I hope
that it may receive the attention it deserves. Perhaps its availability will
at last make the study of articulation and phrasing of correlative
importance to the study of harmony and counterpoint.

                                                    Leigh Gerdine
                                                    Webster College

August 1, 1972

Contents

⋙ ⋙ ⋙ ⋘ ⋘ ⋘

Part One

GENERAL BACKGROUND

Part Two

PHRASING AND ARTICULATION
IN THE WORKS OF BACH, MOZART, AND BEETHOVEN

Abbreviations:

In order to avoid constant interruption of the text with reference to footnotes, in the Bibliography I have given the page number in parentheses (e.g. "on page 25") corresponding to the passages in the text where the author or a work by him is mentioned. It was hoped that this would facilitate the reading of the book without doing injury to its critical or scholarly utility.

Nichts ist drinnen, nichts ist draussen,
denn was innen, das ist aussen
　　　　　(Goethe, *Epirrhema*)

(Nothing is wholly "within" or "without,"
for the interior determines the exterior.)

⤜⤜⤜ ⤜⤜⤜ ⤜⤜⤜ ⤛⤛⤛ ⤛⤛⤛ ⤛⤛⤛

Unfortunately, a work that deals with the question of articulation does not yet exist; moreover, in our time, such a work would give its author insuperable difficulties, for questions about articulation would have to be raised in the context of vocal music, that is to say, with respect to that long lost art of the division of the breath in vocal music which in mysterious fashion still lies at the basis of instrumental articulation.

HEINRICH SCHENKER

PART ONE

꘏꘏ ꘏꘏ ꘏꘏ ꘏꘏ ꘏꘏ ꘏꘏

General Background

CHAPTER ONE

≫≫ ≫≫ ≫≫ ≪≪ ≪≪ ≪≪

The Problem

THIS WORK represents a totally new edition of a book of mine that
appeared thirty years ago, *Die musikalische Artikulation, besonders bei
Joh. Seb. Bach (Musical Articulation, especially in the Works of Johann
Sebastian Bach)*. That book had been out of print for years, but because
it was the only monograph dedicated to this small but important area
of music, many requests had been received for a new edition. If, despite
all its imperfections, my book had in its time a certain effect, that is
perhaps because it was written *from* the practice of music and *for* the
practice of music, and its contents were of significance to every practicing musician: as an organist I played Bach and older masters in part
from unedited editions, in part — it appeared to me — from editions not
always correctly marked from a stylistic point of view; I was trying to
find standards for an objective and authentic manner of performance
suitable to the style of the period. In this quest, it seemed to me that
for older music, articulation was of special significance. My studies led
me in particular to a detailed consideration of the manner of articulation and its expressive possibilities. Out of such studies I compiled a
work more systematically applied than historically based, whose utility
lay chiefly in its application to the performance of the unedited works
of Bach for clavier and organ.

When, after so long a time, I set about to publish this early effort
anew, I became aware that I could not simply rework or improve it,
but that the book must be rewritten from the ground up. Not only has
research made powerful strides in these thirty years, not only have
editors and performers of older music given more attention to questions
of this sort than they once did, but it now appeared to me essential to

include also the correlative area of phrasing with that of articulation. These two areas, so closely related yet so sharply differentiated from one another, illuminate one another; further, since the massive confusion raised fifty years ago by Riemann's *Phrasierungslehre (Grammar of Phrasing)* and his *Phrasierungsausgaben (Phrased Editions)*, this subject had become a hot issue that no one would take hold of, with the result that our conceptions in the whole area of phrasing remained almost no further advanced than they were in Riemann's time. Surprisingly, even up to the present the subject of articulation has remained a stepchild: as a sub-area of musical notation, it certainly ought to be dealt with in the basic works on notation; but the literature on that subject by Johannes Wolf, Riemann, and others mentions articulation either not at all, or very cursorily. Ernst Kurth too in his *Grundlagen des linearen Kontrapunkts (Bases of Linear Counterpoint)*, paid no attention to it whatever, and even cited musical examples from Bach, the autographs of which carry markings, without including them; what is more, in the *Revisionberichten* of the complete editions and *Denkmäler*, one generally finds almost nothing on the various possibilities of articulation (although in recent years this situation has improved).

Greater still is the confusion in the daily parlance of the practicing musician, where concepts of "phrasing" and "articulation" are used interchangeably without distinction. It is the rare musician who can at first attempt define the difference between rhythm and meter, or distinguish precisely between motif and phrase; equally rarely does one find a musician to whom the difference between phrasing and articulation has become entirely clear. In particular, violinists are almost invariably accustomed to speaking of this or that "phrasing" of a passage, identifying bowings with articulation. But the words "phrasing" and "articulation" have basically different meanings: *phrasing* is much like the subdivision of thought; its function is to link together subdivisions of musical thought (phrases) and to set them off from one another; it has thus the same function as punctuation marks in language. "He who phrases incorrectly is like a man who does not understand the language he speaks," said Chopin to his student Mikuli. Hans von Bülow expressed it similarly: "In music, we must punctuate, phrase, separate: we must *play* the piano, not babble." The function of musical *articulation*, on the other hand, is the binding together or the separation of the individual notes; it leaves the intellectual content of a melody line inviolable, but it determines its expression. There is, therefore, as a rule only one possible, thoughtful phrasing, but there are several possibilities of articulation. This clear-cut distinction between articulation and phrasing excludes any possible confusion. There is, however, a border area between the two which I have dealt with here in greater detail than in the first version of this book: the construction of groups through articulation, which some consider to belong more properly in the area of phrasing. To avoid confusion, I have named this phenomenon, which is of particular importance in performing Bach, "the construction of groups through articulation." Especially complicated is the treatment of phrasing in polyphonic music; here the individual voice has not only its individual life — and this must be separately phrased — but all the voices must obey a higher common law, which must also be revealed through the phrasing.

The subtitle of this work, "A Contribution to a Rhetoric of Music," implies that music may be conceived as a language of sound. This is not obvious without further consideration; in precisely what manner this is to be understood will be dealt with in the chapter "The Language of Music," which will lay the basis for a treatment of the areas of phrasing and articulation as the mechanisms of expression of this language of sound.

With this broadening of the problem, the single-purposed concentration upon J. S. Bach was abandoned; however, because of its importance in practice, the chapter on Bach was treated with special completeness, along with those on Mozart and Beethoven. This new edition of the work, too, addresses itself above all to the practicing musician, who wants to think seriously about the bases of his art; it will be especially helpful to him in understanding correctly the sense of the older unmarked music, and in conceiving its expression correctly. Because of the abundance of material, limitation of this work to the most necessary matters became unavoidable. If, in the words of a clever French author, the surest method of being boring is to say everything, one must renounce the tendency to chronicle the historical development of phrasing and articulation in all its detail; further, the musical examples, which form an integral part of the text, will in many cases make long-winded explanations superfluous.

Thus an entirely new edifice is constructed, with broader design, a better-secured foundation, with more and better-ordered rooms. What more could I wish than that musicians go in and out of it, and work to improve it in their turn!

⋙ ⋙ ⋙ ⋘ ⋘ ⋘

CHAPTER TWO

The Language of Music

WE MIGHT think of our whole corpus of music as developing from two ancestral roots, from which it continues to derive its life and strength: from the basic experience of sound for its own sake; and from its association, thousands of years old, with words. The first root reaches deep down into prehistoric times, when music was still experienced as a charm, as magic that would help to ban or to exorcise demons (a final faint relic of which is still with us in the whistles and bangings of New Year's Eve). With the growth of culture and civilization, this sound-experience lost its magical quality, and in its place came first an increasingly intellectual, then an esthetic evaluation of sound, which now was felt to be beautiful, ugly, tender, or fiery, in gradations ever more numerous. Unhindered from any direction, music constructed increasingly its own realm apart from the world of reality, where "facts impinge harshly upon space." Nowadays our definition might be: music is not what we hear, rather what we conceive in what we hear. But the ageless sound-experience is still alive in us too, if a beautiful voice, a true violin tone, the mingling of the tone colors of the orchestra, the full peal of the organ touch us directly; even the highly sophisticated listener cannot avoid this reaction — nor need he be ashamed of it.

"The graphic arts should breathe life; I require spirit from the poet; but the soul speaks only through Polyhymnia." The soul that Schiller here ascribes only to music is not to be taken as musical sound, not even the purest musical sound, but simply and uniquely musical sound in its basic and ever powerful relationship with speech. But then, speech was indeed bound up closely with magic in its beginnings, in the words of priests and kings. Something of this, too, is still alive in the Christian service: in the liturgies, in the prayers and blessings of the priests. But speech, like music, and more quickly than music, was lifted into the spotlight of self-consciousness; it acquired the ability to create concepts, and to make assertions, and it became the most powerful means for men to communicate with each other. The invention of writing made it possible to keep thoughts alive over thousands of years; the effect of its scope was increased a hundredfold through the invention of printing. Printing, that incredible advance, however, brought with itself an impoverishment: the black letters can only convey the sense, not the expression of spoken discourse. As is well known, a question often arises not only about "what I say," but also as well (and sometimes to a greater degree) about "how I say it." With the adage "the inflection makes the music" the French mean not music, but rather a kind of speech in which one may say "yes" in such a manner as to mean "no."

If, then, as the language in daily use was ever more debased through its use as a medium of exchange for men in their petty day-to-day affairs, at the same time all cultures created and preserved a reserved area in which the old purity of the language was still safeguarded, an area that did not need to be sacrificed to necessity: the realm of poetry. Poetry not only safeguards the old, not yet debased linguistic values; it also keeps them alive through the magic of the related, unshakable meter of the verse, through the pleasing sound of rhyme and alliteration, through an artful construction of strophe. But these three elements are gates that stand wide open in the direction of music.

If, in what follows, the subject is "music," only the music of the West is to be understood thereby, for we understand Persian or Chinese music as little as we understand the language of these lands. That we in the West do have a number of national languages, but only one universally understandable language of music (a priceless possession), is to be attributed to the unity of the ancient Western Christian culture, which even the decay of the late Roman Empire could not prevent, but which in the Christian religion, and through religion in music, created a strong bond among the people of the Western cultural area. It was especially the early Christian church music, the so-called Gregorian chant, that knitted this bond so tightly that the unity of Western music has continued to the present day despite all national division. (On the other hand, the highly developed folk music of the Balkans, which for centuries were ruled by the Ottomans, is no longer entirely "our" musical language.)

In language, we distinguish between poetry and prose. It is almost self-evident that the road from language to music leads via poetry. In our Western music, however, strong influences of prose were effective because the music of the Middle Ages was for a thousand years bound up inseparably with the words of the Bible. Because of this, the prose of the Latin Bible translation, the so-called Vulgate, has had an extraordinarily great influence upon the development of music. The imitative polyphonic style of church music of the fifteenth and sixteenth centuries was developed in the composition of Masses and motets on prose texts, and from these arose the ancestors of the instrumental fugue (ricercare, fantasia) and the fugue itself, so that one might designate the fugues of Bach as "composed prose." To recognize this is important for the basis of phrasing of the Bach fugues insofar as the two- or four-measure pattern is not basic for such forms, as it is so helpfully presented to music in dance and song.

The process of a gradual freeing of instrumental music from the word, prepared in the fourteenth and fifteenth centuries and completed with an almost frightening speed in the sixteenth century, neither can nor need be described here in detail. Still more than through this emancipation, music removed itself even further from language when it began to let several voices sound together at the same time under certain specified conditions in that harmonic polyphony through which our Western music distinguishes itself from all other musical cultures of the world. Whether this momentous emancipation signifies a gain, as is generally and rightly concluded, or a lamentable loss of substance, as Wolf and Petersen have advocated in their book *Das Schicksal der Musik von der Antike zur Gegenwart (The Destiny of Music from Ancient Times to the Present)*, is not called into question.

However, the time has come to speak of music itself, and to raise the question: In what manner was this emancipation from the word brought about? This is first to raise the question: Why, truly, does man sing? The answer is given to us by all the high cultures of the earth, whose religious service is sung or in which song plays a meaningful role: the sung performance of the holy text removes the profane everydayness of the language, exalts its expression and safeguards it for centuries through oral transmission and with the help of musical symbols. Never and nowhere are we so directly near to original Christianity as in Gregorian chant or old Christian hymns. We find in Gregorian chant all the stages between language and music: from speech in indefinite pitches through the intensification of expression, grows the measured recitative; from it — according to Jacob Grimm — through further intensification, song. The quiet prayer on a single note (of which Verdi made so gripping a use in his Requiem) is already music. The next step in the development is represented by the so-called psalm-tones, in which the voice is raised to a held note *(tenor)* from which it falls again at the end of every half-verse. Another step presents the simple syllabic melodies in which a melody note falls on every syllable of the text; a further step brings us melismatic, richly decorated melodies (the end of the Alleluia); and from this point on, music could take the final step, that of abandoning the text entirely, in the beautiful words of Jacob Grimm, in order to rise to heights such that no merely verbal thought could follow.

Whether music has succeeded, in the process of this emancipation, in creating its own language is a question that should not be lightly answered. Many thinkers have regarded the distinction between language and music to lie in the fact that it is given to language to make specific assertions, whereas music is destined to express indefinite feelings and experiences, or to indulge in an empty play of form. Musicians, in their turn, are quick to cite quotations, such as the famous one from Beethoven, "Music is a higher revelation than all wisdom and philosophy" (an expression that may not have come from him at all, but was attributed to him by Bettina von Arnim). From all of this one must conclude that it is at least as difficult to posit the pre-eminence of music over poetry as to posit its inferiority. Such violent emotion as a tragedy can evoke in us is not given to music, but music touches areas into which words cannot reach. When a poem is set to music, the music does not express the same thing as did the poem, but it gives expression to something the words alone cannot say.

The mechanisms through which music is expressed are of greater variety and are put together of more heterogeneous elements than are those of language. Apparently only a few of all those who are daily involved with music in some fashion have ever taken this into account. "In the beginning was rhythm": this is as true for poetry as for music; however, music is, above all *sound*, for we can only experience it through the medium of sound. If we take the concept of sound not from the acoustic but from the musical point of view, then the simplest sound is a musical tone, and even a single tone contains a host of distinguishable features. In contrast to noise, it has an identifiable pitch and a definite duration; it is clearly set apart from its neighboring tones, which must lie a given interval from it; it has a specific place in the sound continuum (a higher or a lower note, according to our terminology), it has a particular tone color and a specific (constant or changing) intensity. All of these characteristics have their direct comparisons in language, so that we may correctly conceive the musical (or, more properly, the musically inspired) sound as a speech tone heightened in expression and purified. If several sounds are joined together in a melody or in a melodic line, then the characteristics listed above are

involved as well as the movement of the sounds in the sound continuum, their rise or fall (corresponding to the rise and fall of the speaking
voice, but far beyond its limits), the limitation of the melodic line to
the familiar scale of given intervals (in contrast to the indefiniteness
of pitch change in the speaking voice), the concept of scalewise movement, the leap, the relationship of all sounds of the scale to a basic or
central sound (in language rudimentarily present in the normal speaking voice), the varying quality of the intervals (here at last the analogy
to language breaks down). Tempo is also derivable from speech,
although in music it has become refined as well as extended far beyond
the boundaries of speech.

At any rate, phrasing and articulation as attributes of the melodic
line are the two areas to which this work is dedicated. The first of
these, phrasing, can only be understood by analogy to language; the
second, articulation, is to be understood not exclusively but chiefly
through the same analogy. Again, new complicating elements entered
as Western music began to develop its polyphony: concepts such as
consonance and dissonance (rudimentarily present already in mono-
phonic music), tonality, modulation, character of the keys, and others;
but these cannot be given consideration within the limitation of this
work.

The essential meaning of a melody is not changed through a livelier
or slower tempo, through a varying of loudness or tone color, through
a transfer of octave higher or lower, through a transposition to another
key, nor even through an alteration in articulation. Suppose one were
to amuse himself by taking a theme, such as the first in the *Sonata
facile* (K.545) by Mozart, and altering it in terms of all of these possibilities — the most comical distortions of expression will arise in this
fashion, but the essential meaning of the theme remains the same. However, the melodic meaning is changed immediately if specific melodic
steps are altered (in language, if other words be substituted), or if an
accent is misplaced (in speech, for example, should one read *cónsum-
mate* in place of *consúmmate*), and if it is incorrectly phrased (in
speech if the punctuation marks be changed).

From the parallel drawn, it is obvious that in music too we are
justified in distinguishing between meaning and expression, a fact that
demonstrates at least a close relationship between music and language.
The fact is that we express ourselves in music in order to be understood
(more correctly: to be understood by the members of our cultural com-
munity) with the same certainty as we express ourselves in language.
Hanslick put this strikingly: "A theme of Mozart or Beethoven stands
as securely and independently upon its own feet as a verse of Goethe,

an epigram of Lessing, a statue of Thorwaldsen, or a painting by Over-beck. The independent musical thoughts [themes] have the precision of a quotation and the vividness of a painting; they are individual, personal, external." An important distinction ought not be overlooked, however: although one can indeed memorize a sonata as well as a poem, one cannot translate a piece of music, as one can translate foreign literature. This is important because it shows that the relationship between meaning and expression in music is differently proportioned than it is in language. In language, even in the boldest, freest poem, the meaning will always stand in first place; the meaning outlines the contours, the shading is given by the delivery (the expression). In music on the other hand, especially in the newer music, this situation is often reversed so that the expressive elements (tone color, tempo, dynamics, articulation) affect us more powerfully than does the content of the specific theme. Therefore it follows that in music not much is accomplished with a simple conveyance of the content. Bülow formulated this tellingly: "A merely pure, merely correct performance is worth only as much as a spelling in sound. It belongs with the rudiments. Clear enunciation is still not understandable declamation; meaningful declamation is still not sensitive and therefore expressive eloquence. An art of performance in musical language must above all be grounded in the working together of these three factors, in which each higher element depends upon the lower."

In the presence of these many factors of such different natures, it is obvious that musical scholarship has an incomparably more difficult problem to master than has linguistic scholarship in its area, and it ought not to surprise us that musicologists have not yet completely solved the problem. Valuable attempts in that direction have been made by the thoughtful but not easily readable book by Jacques Handschin, *Der Toncharakter (The Character of Sound)*. To date, only two important areas in music, harmony and counterpoint (the study of melody), have been thoroughly explored, albeit chiefly from the point of view of musical practice. Both areas are taught mostly as a craft study for the beginning musician: in the study of harmony, the student discovers how chords are built and how they are connected to one another; but of their expressive significance, even of such strong and characteristic dissonances as the so-called Neapolitan sixth chord or the diminished seventh chord, there is no mention in the average harmony text. The situation is similar in the teaching of counterpoint, where the devices of part-writing are customarily taught as the observance of certain laws and proscriptions; but both laws and proscriptions are generally arbitrarily set up without any further justification than that this or that progression "sounds bad" (or may have sounded bad in earlier practice). Still less have the countless changing relationships of all of these areas been explored. To mention only the simplest examples, who has not been annoyed to find, in traditional harmony, fleshless chords bound together, when in reality it is the melody that implies their relationship; or to find students of counterpoint being advised to exclude harmonic thinking as much as possible, in order to "feel" in an entirely linear fashion? Thus very significant questions which can only be resolved if the individual areas make their own contribution, await a future musical grammar. We lack studies on the development and change of harmonic thought, on the development and gradual transformation of the rules of part-writing, monographs on tempo, or dynamics, or tone color in their significance and development in Western music.

For the two areas of phrasing and articulation the following work seeks to make some contribution. The preconditions for it are relatively favorable, because these two areas are easily isolated and infringe little upon other areas; and at the same time both are especially suited to support the evidence that one may in fact speak of a "language of music" without being guilty of dealing with vague and deceptive figures of speech.

➤➤ ➤➤ ➤➤ ◄◄ ◄◄ ◄◄

CHAPTER THREE

Fundamentals of Phrasing

IN VIEW of the present confusion of terminology, it is necessary, before we can deal effectively with phrasing, to establish the concept of what a phrase is. By a musical phrase here shall be understood the equivalent of a line of verse in poetry, or of a simple unbroken sentence in prose. "In the beginning was the sentence," concluded the linguistic philosopher Mauthner: only through a gradual, ever farther-reaching differentiation were the individual words with their various functions formed out of an originally compact sound-expression with the meaning of a whole sentence, and the construction of sentences was made possible — from the simplest sentence, such as children write in their letters ("How are you? I am fine!") to the most involved sentence structures such as we often encounter in philosophy, especially with Kant. In order to join or to separate the parts of sentences, the West has made use of certain reading signs (punctuation marks). Antiquity did not know them, nor did the early Middle Ages; one read aloud in order to make the sense clear, and in writing one crowded together more closely those parts of a sentence that belonged together. Only in the course of the Middle Ages were indications of punctuation introduced and proliferated bit by bit: the period (a colon), the oblique stroke with the meaning of a semicolon or comma, later changed via abbreviation to the comma, the question mark, comma and period combined as semicolon, the colon, the exclamation point, the parenthesis (for subsidiary interpolation), the dash — for coordinate interpolation — periods, to show an implied continuation . . . also doubled symbols such as ?! and !! (corresponding to *ff* in music) — from these gradually arose a rich arsenal of supplementary indications that has been adequate for all present requirements. The most important of these serve the purpose of clarifying the sense; certain others, such as the exclamation point, beyond the sense, clarify the expression; they suggest to the reader something that cannot truly be expressed through the written material. It is indeed not possible with the help of written signs to bring to expression the strength of sound or the color, the tempo, or the rhythm of the spoken word. The comic element in the sentence "Boom, boom, roared the cannon, but much louder" is founded precisely in this impossibility. The punctuation signs show the reader when and how he should breathe in a living performance. This is by no means negligible: through the breath, those things that pertain to one another are brought together in a unity and set off from what follows: between major subdivisions, one breathes deeply; between smaller subdivisions, one breathes only a little. Thus is breath, the spirit of man, bound together in a mysterious manner with the spirit of language; and we understand that the Greeks had the same word for breath as they had for soul (*pneuma*). As in language, so in music, "to phrase" means equally "to breathe"; "to phrase well" means "to breathe intelligently."

Everything language cannot express with the help of punctuation signs — height and depth of pitch, duration, tempo, dynamics, rhythm, articulation — music is able to bring to expression through its notational system and additional signs, although, in most curious fashion, music has refused to create for itself a system of punctuation marks similar to that of language. We may well feel in music a little interruption, such as the comma — but it is not indicated; we recognize, especially in the newer music, countless questioning turns of expression, for example, in Richard Wagner's *Götterdämmerung:*

but there is no question mark in music. The ceaseless repetition of the fortissimo strokes at the end of Beethoven's Fifth Symphony has the effect of the exclamation point (Victory! Victory!), but music has no sign for it. In the connections in Classical music created by the "attacca" — as a prime example, in the connection from the third to the fourth movements of Beethoven's Fifth Symphony — we feel colons, but we must imagine them. An attempt was made at least once to introduce speech punctuation into music; Professor Jacob Fischer, a Viennese, prepared a "punctuated edition" of Classical works in 1926; but this has remained only an experiment (it would be a strange thing indeed to find question marks, exclamation points, and colons in a sonata of Beethoven!).

More complicated than in prose is the question of the subdivision of sense in poetry, where the verse as an organizing principle generally takes precedence over the sentence. This is already expressed visually by the fact that with every verse a new line begins, so that the eye is compelled to conceive the verse as a unit. It therefore follows that the construction of verse and the construction of sentence can come into conflict with one another. The line that runs on into the next line, the so-called *enjambement,* appears early in art-poetry, but rarely occurs in true folk song, in which sentence structure and verse structure generally coincide:

> Vom Himmel hoch da komm ich her
> ich bring euch gute neue Mär
> der guten Mär bring ich so viel
> davon ich sing'n und sagen will.

> From heaven on high to earth I come
> I bring you good new tidings
> of good tidings I bring so much
> of which I will sing and tell.

Music always follows the higher organizational pattern of the text, and the effect is uncommonly ugly therefore when, in a folk song or in a hymn, the entire congregation must breathe in the middle of a phrase. Even in the polyphonic works of the sixteenth century, the lines of the cantus firmus are clearly separated, and with great sensitivity the musical separation expresses their greater or lesser speech separation. Art music must similarly be prepared to deal with the run-on line; if it does not, as in the aria from *Der Freischütz:*

> Trübe Augen
> Liebchen taugen
> einem holden
> Bräutchen nicht,

there result unintentional comic effects. Just as intolerable, of course, is the opposite extreme, which one finds in many modern songs, where the verse construction is often totally destroyed in favor of the sentence structure; it is a token of the great mastery of Brahms as a *Lieder* composer that in this conflict he knew how to find the proper middle ground.

If both the art music of earlier centuries and the great masters of music have left it to the interpreter to find his own proper phrasing, on pedagogic grounds attempts have been made to indicate phrasing. The earliest such signs are to be found in Gregorian chant, where the subdividing strokes of the text are early inserted into the music as well. Three types of subdividing strokes are used in modern Gregorian notation: the *divisio major,* a double line drawn through the staff at the end of a sentence; the *divisio minor,* a single line drawn through the staff at the end of a period; and the *divisio minima,* a half-line at the end of a phrase.° Often however, particularly in long melismas that exceed the limitations of a single breath, it is left to the singer to find a suitable caesura for taking a breath. In French organ music of about 1700, one frequently finds the double stroke to indicate the transfer of manual from the *Grand Clavier* to the *Positif.*

For the indication of points of greater rest, toward the end of the Middle Ages the fermata ⌒ (corona) was introduced, a sign that lies like a bell over the note to be held, and that brings the motion to a halt. The fermata might appear at the end of whole movements (as of a motet), as well as of subsections (as within the Gloria of a Mass). We find a remarkable use of the fermata in Dufay, who in the last line of his motet, *Alma redemptoris mater,* placed a fermata over every single note (much in the sense of a *molto ritenuto*). Toward the end of the seventeenth century, the fermata was adopted to indicate the ends of lines in the Lutheran chorale; how the fermata should be understood in the works of Bach will be dealt with in Chapter 7. The Viennese Classical composers use the fermata frequently also for declamatory interruptions of the motion within a movement, as for example Beethoven at the beginning of the Piano Sonata, Opus 31, No. 3, or of the Trio, Opus 1, No. 3, or in the *Kreutzer Sonata,* and in many other places. In the *Kreutzer,* many players misunderstand not only the fermata, but also the "Adagio" superscript set alongside; they bring the motion to a complete standstill, instead of slowing it down only a little and pausing slightly on the fermata; the pulsating tension of the whole movement ought here to be relaxed a little.

The first breathing signs in secular music appear only at the beginning of the seventeenth century, in Cavalieri's *Rappresentazione di anima e di corpo,* in the following form: ≠ (Schering, p. 183). In the Görlitz Tablature Book of 1650, which contains 100 simple chorale

---

° The Vatican Edition of the Roman chant adds to these a fourth type: a short stroke through the top line of the staff, indicating a short sustaining of the voice and permitting, if necessary, the taking of a very short breath. — Translator.

settings, Scheidt separates the lines through written-out rests; Schütz, however, writes in the foreword to the chorale settings of the Cornelius Becker Psalter (1628) that he "wished to indicate the pauses with a little stroke at the end of every verse [that is, of every line], instead of with rests, because in compositions of this character the rests are of course not really observed" — a significant observation showing that he wished to leave to the performer larger or smaller separations of the line according to the sense and expression. In the *Exequien* (1636) he writes double strokes (//) where the chorus stops singing.

The examples mentioned thus far concerned only single-voiced or homophonic music. In polyphonic music the rest was and remains the only mechanism for phrasing. It is one of the oldest and most important principles of composition in the strict style to emphasize thematic entrances of a voice more markedly through a rest that precedes the entry; the remaining phrase divisions were determined through a detailed study of the words, and were derived for the most part *sui generis* out of the text; in long phrases, breathing was done either according to motivic segments or simply according to need.

The whole corpus of instrumental music remained entirely without indication of phrasing until the beginning of the eighteenth century. There were also the caesuras either indicated through rests or performed according to an analogy with vocal music. The first composer (and the only one among the great composers) who tried to indicate precise phrasing through notation was Couperin.

In the foreword to the third of his four books of *Pièces de Clavecin*, to which the four *Concerts Royaux* are appended (published in 1722), he writes:

> You will encounter a new sign, which looks like this: ' ; it is to mark the end of melodies or of what we call harmonic phrases, and to make it clear that it is necessary to detach slightly the end of a melody before passing on to what follows. The separation is almost imperceptible in general, although in not finding this little silence, persons of taste would know that there was something lacking in the performance; in a word, it is the difference between those who read on and on [without punctuating orally] and those who stop at the periods and commas. These silences should be made to be felt without altering the rhythm.°

° On trouvera un signe nouveau dont voici la figure ' ; c'est pour marquer la terminaison des Chants ou de nos Phrases harmoniques, et pour faire comprendre qu'il faut un peu separer la fin d'un Chant avant de passer à celuy qui suit. Cela est presque imperceptible en general, quoy qu'en n'observant pas ce petit Silence les personnes de goût sentent qu'il manque quelque chose à l'éxécution, en un mot, c'est la diférence de ceux qui lisent de suite, avec ceux qui s'arrêtent aux points et aux virgules. Ces silences se doivent faire sentir sans alterer la mesure.

With these words, truly French in clarity and felicity of expression, the problem of phrasing for instrumental music is opened up in such a way that the whole rationalistic eighteenth century could no longer ignore it. The places Couperin marked with these apostrophes, of which he thought himself the discoverer, are of special interest. He loves groups of 1 + 1 + 2 measures, as in the 20th *Ordre* of the Fourth Book (the ornaments are omitted):

and in the same place, in the *Air dans le goût Polonais*, we find phrasing and the most delicate articulation together:

Occasionally, he marks even the smallest sections with an apostrophe (Third Book):

In the following example (Fourth Book) the breaking of the beam signifies an almost imperceptible separation, the apostrophe a clearer one:

Now Germany entered the scene. Mattheson, in his *Kern melodischer Wissenschaft (The Essence of Melodic Science)*, 1737, fifth section, "Von den Einschnitten der Klangrede" ("On the Subdivisions of Musical Language"), was the first theorist to speak of phrasing, which he called "the most striking and up to the present time, the least considered area." He compared the punctuation of language with the parts of the human body: the period with a whole member (the arm), the semi-colon with a half-member (the elbow), the comma with a joint (the wrist), and he distinguished "total" and "suspended" commas: the latter are felt, but are not notated because of their slightness. If an element of punctuation were there only for emotional effect (for example, "Ah!"), then the composer ought not be misled into making a caesura.

In 1767, Jean Jacques Rousseau defined musical punctuation in his *Dictionnaire de Musique* as "the making perceptible of the more or less complete points of rest and the separation of the phrases in such a manner that one feels in their inflection as well as in their cadences the beginning, fall, and greater or lesser connections just as one feels all of these with the help of punctuation in speech."

In 1774, J. P. A. Schulz suggested in his article on "Performance" in Sulzer's *Theorie der schönen Künste (Theory of the Fine Arts)* that the beginning of a phrase should be indicated with a little cross (+), the end with a little circle (o). He illustrates this in the following example:

and he remarks:

> Thus it would be highly erroneous if one were, for example, to perform the sixth measure in such a manner as though the phrase began with the first note, when indeed the preceding phrase ends with it, as the eighth rest of the preceding measure shows. . . . It is unbelievable how formless and lacking in clarity melody becomes if the caesuras are incorrect or not taken into account. To convince himself of this, one need only to perform a gavotte in such a manner that the caesuras in the middle of the measure are not observed. Easy as this dance is to understand, through such a procedure it becomes incomprehensible to everyone. Here again, most often a mistake is made in those places where the phrases begin in the middle of the measure, and indeed on an unaccented beat, because people are generally accustomed to observe only the strong beats of the measure, on which the various accents of the melody fall, and to let the weak beats go by as if they were only cursory.

One notes that whereas Couperin was still writing for an aristocratic public, the North German clavier pedagogues of the eighteenth century were turning to a middleclass public, to whom an elementary conception of taste had first to be introduced.

The two signs suggested by Schulz were (fortunately) not accepted; Daniel Gottlob Türk, who introduced the small vertical stroke of separation $\equiv$ in his *Klavierschule oder Anweisung zum Klavierspielen* (*Clavier School, or Instruction in Clavier Playing*, published in 1789, second edition 1802), had greater success. He uses it for the most part as a double stroke — as a single stroke, the twentieth century has taken it up again.

Türk handled the cases in which a phrase began with an upbeat with special care. Important points of rest are "apparent even to the least sensitive person ... but a far greater alertness and a much finer sensitivity are required to spot the caesura immediately if it falls on an unaccented (especially somewhat short) note." One recognizes these caesuras easily enough if "one pays attention to whether a piece begins with a downbeat, or whether and how many beats, divisions of a beat, and so forth appear every time in the anacrusis. ... For example, if a piece begins with an eighth note on an upbeat, not only will the remaining periods commonly begin the same way, but also the caesura will begin with the last eighth note of the measure." (The whole section "On performance" is quoted in Harich-Schneider, pp. 105ff.) To clarify this, Türk recommends the breaking of the beams and gives the following example:

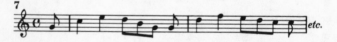

From this we become acquainted with a new means of phrasing, especially of smaller segments, as simple as it is important, which we encountered as early as in the music of Couperin, and which was later used by Bach (see Examples 75, 78 and 79) and especially frequently by Beethoven (Example 32). In his *Phrased Editions* (see Examples 59 and 60) Riemann used it excessively.

The great composers did not make use of the symbols suggested by Couperin, Schulz, Türk, and others; indeed they took no notice of these experiments; curiously, neither did the editors of older music (in the nineteenth century), who preferred to make the beginning and end of a phrase recognizable in general, as Beethoven and the Romantics had done, by means of slurs and performance indications, without going further into the problem. Only the fermata retained its place, especially in the chorale books, where it had the unhealthy effect of slowing down still further the congregational singing of chorales, which since the eighteenth century had been dragging increasingly. In the eighteenth century and well into the nineteenth, it was the task of organists to "beautify" and fill up the overlong fermatas between lines with excessively florid interpolations. No wonder that, in recent decades, when an attempt was successfully made to enliven congregational singing again, the fermata was removed, and was replaced either by a single or a double stroke. In instrumental music too, the stroke indicating a separation was made use of again about 1900 by Theodor Wiehmayer in his instructive editions of Classical piano works. He used a larger stroke with the meaning of a semicolon and a smaller stroke as a comma, both unfortunately as well in cases that were already quite clear or where other phrase linkages would have been both possible and conceivable. Only the smaller stroke of separation endured; I have made use of it in my editions of old organ music (Frescobaldi, Scheidt, Buxtehude, Lübeck) but I am quite aware that it may be regarded as only a pedagogic aid, a mechanism which the great majority of players will nevertheless find necessary for a long time. In a new edition of the Buxtehude volume, I have again removed a number of these small indications — I perceived that I had fallen into the same error as Wiehmayer. With such "aids" the situation is entirely comparable to that of commentaries on the classics: in the case of Goethe (if we are not dealing with Part II of *Faust*) we are annoyed by obtrusive commentary ("here Goethe is in error"); in the case of Dante's *Divine Comedy*, on the other hand, a commentary is indispensable to most readers.

IRREGULARITIES IN THE CONSTRUCTION OF PHRASES
AND IN PHRASING

So far only the simplest case was considered, namely that in which the phrases are completely separated from one another, and where this separation should be made perfectly clear. Music recognizes, however, a host of complications in phrase structure that affect phrasing, conflicting aspects that have no parallel in language. Among them are the following: a) phrase-end concealment, b) phrase linkage, c) phrase elision, and d) phrase overlapping.

a) *Phrase-end concealment* occurs when the boundary between two phrases is deliberately effaced (an example of this is to be observed in Baroque architecture in the intentional effacing of important structural supports), or when the boundary between two phrases is bridged over.

Both types are especially frequently found in Mozart, for example the obliteration of the boundary between two phrases in the Sonata K. 333:

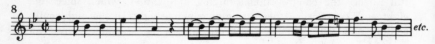

and the bridging of the boundary between two phrases in the Rondo K. 494:

The square brackets indicate the phrase limits; in some editions (for example, Peters) the editors have arbitrarily so altered Mozart's phrasings that they agree with the brackets given here. In the manuscript of the A-minor Rondo (K. 511) Mozart at first permitted the first half of the theme to end in the normal fashion, on G♯, then he crossed out the slur and continued it to E:

which now gives the theme a charm of an entirely individual sort. In Beethoven's Sonata, Opus 31, No. 2, as in Chopin's Mazurka, Opus 6, No. 3, a "false" sixth arises in this fashion, playful in the case of Beethoven, coquettish in that of Chopin:

It is a sign of the touching uprightness of Türk that he holds things of this sort to be inadmissible. He is of the opinion that "In the next example, the execution indicated by the slur is . . . logically incorrect":

"It should sound like this":

b)   A *phrase linkage* arises when the first phrase ends with the beginning note of the next. This is almost the rule in the exposition of a fugue, where the newly entering voice comes in upon the final note of the first, and thus does not permit the motion to come to rest. In symphonic music, this phenomenon is especially easily perceptible if the two phrases are divided between various instruments, as in Beethoven's First Symphony:

For Beethoven, this technique is especially characteristic. In the following example (Trio, Opus 1, No. 3) the first four phrases follow one another entirely regularly ($2 + 2 + 2 + 3$ measures); then, however, there enters a phrase linkage imposed through dynamic accents (see the brackets). Without this element of force, one would have taken the G in the eleventh measure of the example as marking the end of a phrase, and the eighth notes of F, E♭ as the beginning, just as in measures 13 and 15 one hears the new phrase begin on the second eighth note:

This impression of a new beginning can also arise through a sudden diminuendo, as in Brahms's Violin Sonata in A major, Opus 100, where in the fifth measure, without the notation "piano," one might have felt the beginning of the phrase only at the three eighth notes:

c)   A *phrase elision* arises if the abrupt change is so strong that the final tone of the first phrase is no longer heard, as on the E♭ in the first movement of Beethoven's Trio, Opus 1, No. 3:

d) *Phrase overlapping* of two (or more) phrases is known to every musician from the stretto of the fugue; fine examples are furnished by the first fugue of the *Well-Tempered Clavier*. Phrase overlapping almost always requires the presence of two or more voices; especially charming are those rare cases where it is encountered in a single voice. This is what happens in the C-minor Fugue of Volume I of the *Well-Tempered Clavier*, where the half measure that ends the sequence of the episode, indicated by brackets, is also the beginning of the subject (as is later established):

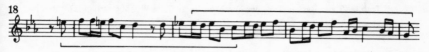

A similar instance occurs in the Scherzo of the *Eroica*, when the violin begins with an eight-measure phrase; the oboe's answer already overlaps this phrase, however, in measures 7 and 8:

As soon as one has learned to notice all these conflicting details of structure, one will recognize them, and will be able to take account of them in performance. There are cases, however, in which the living music has so been forced into the Procrustean bed of the barline that a sensible reading is scarcely possible in a strictly metronomic performance, for every pause, even the tiniest breath, requires a certain amount of time which cannot always be spared from the preceding note.

Thus in the Bach motet *Jesu, meine Freude*, every choral director has surely found how difficult it is to make the third strophe, *Trotz dem alten Drachen*, comprehensible. If Bach's stubborn accentuation be — or might be — performed with the measures strongly accented, the following caricature would emerge:

Trotz dem alten Drachen Trotz!
Trotz des Todes Rachen Trotz!
Trotz der Furcht dazu Tobe!

Tobe Welt und springe ich,
steh' hier und singe in
gar sichrer Ruh°

Trotz,   Trotz dem al _ ten Dra _ chen, Trotz dem alten Drachen, Trotz, Trotz des To _ des Ra _

chen, Trotz des Todes Rachen, Trotz der Furcht da _ zu! To be Welt und springe, ich steh hier

The breath pause to be inserted after the unison passages here should
have at least the duration of an eighth note.

In the Brahms D-minor Piano Concerto, the concluding theme of the
first movement is the following:

Only if the horn player sets off the theme correctly through the finest
dynamic and agogic shading will he prevent it from being heard in the
following distorted fashion:

°For the English-speaking reader the absurdity of this misreading may not be
immediately apparent. The sense, of course, is the following:

Trotz dem alten Drachen,
Trotz des Todes Rachen,
Trotz der Furcht dazu:
Tobe, Welt, und springe;
ich steh' hier und singe
in gar sich'rer Ruh.

— Translator.

Similarly in the *Pathétique Sonata* when, without the observance of the caesura indicated here, the *sforzando* halfnote C is heard (unfortunately, how often!) as the end of the first half phrase:

From the Bagatelles of Beethoven two contrasted examples are shown. In the Bagatelle, Opus 126, No. 4, the melody leaps as if into an abyss:

Here a certain amount of time, though ever so small, must be left to the fall. At the end of the Bagatelle, Opus 119, No. 1 the performer must clearly separate from one another the various qualities of the two G's in measure three:

The first G creates a cadence, through a delayed suspension; the second begins the coda. Here also an almost imperceptible caesura must come to the aid of the hearer's conception.

PHRASING THROUGH EXTENSION

Next to the chief problem of phrasing, that of separating phrases clearly from one another, lies the scarcely less important second problem, that of extending them. To indicate this, an obvious solution would have been to utilize the slur, which could span the entire phrase visually. From such a use, however, arise inevitable conflicts with the meaning of the slur as a legato mark; one and the same symbol cannot

be used indiscriminately with two separate meanings. Riemann tried
to do it, but his attempt was unsuccessful. Until very recently, studies
in form and analysis have sought to create symbols to make clear the
unity of a phrase. Here again Riemann must be named as the pioneer,
for he introduced into his formal analyses, as well as in his *Phrased
Editions,* measure numbers (1-8, 1-4). He took the eight-measure unit
as the norm and, in numbering the measures, showed deviations from
the norm in a method as ingenious as it was simple: repetitions, especially in the conclusive cadential passages so frequently encountered in
Beethoven, were designated by a letter set beside the number (e.g., 7a,
8a, if the two last measures were repeated; 8b, 8c, if the last measure
alone was repeated twice); irregularities in phrase construction he
designated by a reinterpretation of the number of measures (3 = 5).
Unfortunately this system has two serious flaws: the first arises from the
fact that for Riemann one measure was equivalent to another measure.
Measures may, however, be of very different lengths, and the general
analytic purpose cannot be served without the distinction suggested by
Wiehmayer between normal-sized measures and large and small measures. Two large measures may have the same content as eight small
ones — the number of measures alone, then, cannot be used for the
measurement of phrases and periods. The other objection that must be
raised is that not all music can be forced into a pointless schema of eight
measures. In particular, polyphonic music does not permit this, so that
nothing of any use in its interpretation comes from Riemann. It must
nevertheless be granted that Riemann's system has shown itself to be
very fruitful, especially as applied to song and dance forms; even Anton
Bruckner in the sketches for the finale (unfinished) of his Ninth Symphony placed the numbers 1 − 4, 1 − 6, 1 − 8, under the first 18 measures (facsimile in MGG, cols. 373/374). In the place of Riemann's
numbering of measures, Theodor Wiehmayer, in his *Musikalische
Rhythmik und Metrik,* used the numbering of "sound feet" (as, in
poetry, of "metric feet"), and with this has established a firm basis for
formal analysis.

    In recent years, a practicing musician has once more joined with
Riemann: the pianist Artur Schnabel, in his edition of Brahms's three
Violin Sonatas (Peters). He indicates only the irregularities of the
phrase construction by means of Roman numerals placed underneath
the notes; where there is no indication, the player must rely upon a
normal four-measure unit. The opening of the A-major Violin Sonata,
in which the violin each time repeats the last measure of the four-
measure phrase with which the piano begins, he designates at the

beginning with I, at the close with V (Riemann would here have indicated, more adroitly, 1 — 4 and 4a):

This experiment has been little noted: its advantage is its simplicity and the lack of violence done to the musical structure; its disadvantage, that complications of phrase structure, such as phrase linkage and phrase overlapping — particularly important elements in the music of Brahms — cannot be expressed in this fashion.

THE PHRASING OF LARGE SECTIONS

The concluding discussion here will be concerned with the setting off of larger sections with respect to one another. One would like not to return to the word "phrasing" to express this, but there is no other term known; and if phrasing in one sense is the sense-grouping of notes, then the meaningful grouping of larger sections is as important as phrasing in the more restricted sense. The large caesuras are indeed, as Türk observed, "apparent even to the least sensitive person," and yet in musical practice they are often accorded shamefully little attention. Beyond the phrase, in music, lies the period, as in poetry beyond the verse lies the strophe, and in prose, beyond the clause the complete sentence. The larger forms in music — the longer song forms, the rondo, the sonata form — correspond to the poem that consists of several strophes, to the prose work that consists of a number of sentences. The cyclic forms, such as the suite, sonata, symphony, correspond to a cycle of sonnets, to an epic form consisting of several cantos; in prose, to a novelette or novel consisting of several chapters. Everyone who recites aloud will, in the performance of these small, larger, or large sections, take each into account and observe it precisely according to its importance; even the reader will insert between larger segments a thoughtful pause, in which he thinks over once again the previously read material before he reads on — only in music has the feeling for this atrophied increasingly.

The adage "rests are music too" has, however, its deep justification. An artist must recognize all shading, from the almost imperceptible separation to the long pause experienced by him and to be recognized by the hearer, and, further, must master them in performance. How rarely, however, is this requirement fulfilled! The great conductors are almost the only ones who understand it. How often does it happen that in variations, especially in sonatas and in chamber music works, the double bars between the individual variations are simply ignored, so that not only do the variations follow one another senselessly without breath pause, but no caesura is made even before the beginning of the first variation to say to the hearer, "Now the theme is finished, now the variations begin!" One finds the same thing in the sequence of minuet (or scherzo) — trio — minuet. Here, if the composer has written no transition or repeat between the movements, at least a measure's pause (or thereabouts) should be introduced between these three parts, if their formal self-sufficiency is not to suffer severely. Still greater should be the pause between the first and second movements of a sonata, while that between the third and fourth can generally be shorter. Often it is simply stage fright that forces the player to go further as quickly as possible. In the twentieth century, however, the cause is perhaps the giddy tempo of life, which carries over into music and is the peculiarly identifying characteristic of mechanical music: the long-playing record, whose total playing surface must be used up, and still more the radio, with its announcements computed on the duration of seconds, true performances by the clock!° It is true that we no longer require pauses of the length favored by the generation of our fathers and grandfathers. With the general intensification of the tempo of life, our ability to react to music has become quicker too, but it would be an irreplaceable loss if the thoughtful pause were to disappear entirely. Earlier generations had a very fine feeling for it; there is an example in Liszt, when at the end of the first part of his *Bénédiction de Dieu dans la solitude* he asks for a "lunga pausa," which he designated in the original edition through an empty half-page with scattered diagonal dots to indicate a silent continuation; Gustav Mahler wrote in the score at the end of the first movement of his Second Symphony, "Here follows a pause of at least five minutes" (!). The Classical composers marked those places in which no pause should be admitted explicitly with the word "attacca" and thus called attention to the fact that in all other cases a pause should be made. And we? Do we no longer have for it "the least sensitivity" of which Türk speaks?

° The author uses an untranslatable pun here: *"Uhr-Aufführungen"* (perform-ances by the clock) for *"Uraufführungen"* (first performances). — Translator.

※» ※» ※» «« «« ««

Fundamentals of Articulation

As WITH PHRASING, we can derive principles of musical articulation from language. The sounds of speech are composed of the sounds that can be made independently: the vowels and the consonants that accompany them. To bring these out clearly and to separate them from one another is the task of speech articulation. The child learns to speak as he learns to articulate. Everyone knows examples of especially difficult articulation with which people amuse themselves in company, as for example "She sells seashells by the seashore" and other such "études," as one would say in music. Furthermore, above all, articulation serves to convey expression insofar as in emotional language the sounds of speech are separated. "The tone of one who is sad is weak and tremulous, the expression short and slow . . . trembling broken-off sounds express fear and anxiety," wrote Krause, one of the founders and the esthetician of the first Berlin school of *Lied*-writers (1753). But the man who sings to himself makes separations too; and in a meaningless question: "You — have — done — that?" the syllables are just as individually ejaculated as in a curtly given command.

It is obvious that in singing, articulation will be done just as in speech. The first references to articulation in singing are to be found as early as in the neumatic notation of the tenth century, where instructions were given to singers through abbreviations both for performance and for articulation (t = *tenere*, co = *conjunguntur*, see Haas p. 42). That the richly decorated melodies of Gregorian chant and the virtuoso organa of the Notre Dame school were articulated in a great variety of ways is obvious; but it is not until the sixteenth century that we find a true choral articulation in the refrains of choral songs by

Gastoldi, Donati, Hassler, Morley, and others with their "la, la, las" or "fa, la, las"; in Lassus's famous serenade of the German mercenary, *Matona mia cara*, the plucking of the lute is imitated with "don-don-don"; in an Italian frottola, the chirping of crickets and in Marenzio's madrigals, fear and trembling are expressed tonally. Naturally, all of this remains without musical annotation; it is not until later and only in individual instances that signs of articulation were carried over from instrumental music to vocal music: we find coloratura arias marked with slurs and dots in Leopold Mozart, in Graupner and others, and also of course in the works of W. A. Mozart. Still rarer is choral articulation, as in the laughing chorus in Handel's *L'Allegro, il Pensieroso ed il Moderato* and in Bach's Cantata No. 102 *(Du schlägest sie, aber sie fühlen es nicht,* see Example 92). That choral articulation sometimes became excessive (and, need we say that today it still occasionally becomes excessive?) we discover from the joking remark of Demantius in 1656 (see Haas, p. 47) over the shaking of the heads of the choir-boys, who sing "Cantahahahahahata" instead of "Cantata"!

We shall limit ourselves in what follows to instrumental articulation, about which something basic may be said, before a short historical section will be given on the development of articulation up to the end of the eighteenth century. The feeling for the variety of expressive possibilities of articulation arose and grew in the seventeenth and eighteenth centuries nearly simultaneously with the feeling for tempo and dynamics. But whereas these latter elements relate to music as a whole, articulation is to be viewed as a function of melody.

For our conception of articulation, therefore, the conception we have of melody is of decisive importance. We follow the well-known definition of Ernst Kurth (in his *Grundlagen des linearen Kontrapunkts, Bases of Linear Counterpoint*): "Melody is a flowing power. . . . Whatever it is that is melodic is based upon the movement through the notes, not in the individual notes through which it streams, and in their ordering from one to another." This definition, which is proposed penetratingly in countless variations in Kurth's book, does not however agree precisely with the manifold character of the musical events. The conception of the melody as a simple progression of movement conflicts with the individual melody note, which as an individual event must be taken as a law unto itself. Not in the unconditional superiority of one principle, as Kurth would have it, but in the conflict of two principles is the character of melody to be understood. At one extreme, the individual existence of the individual note can be almost extinguished, as at the beginning of the Chromatic Fantasy of Bach, which is only stormy movement, or in the *Minute Waltz* of Chopin; at the other extreme, in a pithy, weighty theme, the importance of the individual notes may be felt more strongly than the stream of melody flowing through them, as in the subject of the C♯-minor Fugue (*Well-Tempered Clavier,* Vol. 1) or at the beginning of the *Midsummer Night's Dream Overture* of Mendelssohn, where, under the fermatas, the melodic contour of the upper voice is recognizable as a delicate silver streak:

Between these two extremes lie innumerable gradations; in each one, the battle between line and individual note is fought over again; often enough, articulation steps into this battle, and decides it.

THE LEGATO

It is significant that the words "legato" and "religion" have the same root: *religare* = to bind. Just as Schleiermacher defined religion as the absolute dependency upon and connection of the individual to God, so too is legato in music the symbol of connectedness, of preservation, indeed of completeness, or of humility before music. Only in legato playing does the flow of melody gush forth without finding resistance, without dissipating some of its flowing strength in passage through the notes, which welcome it and lead it further, retreating humbly into the background: thus the legato is the only conflict-free expression of the melodic line, and from the beginning it was restricted to the sacred spheres. The "flowing style" in composition, as in performance, signified the ideal church style, whose classic model we recognize in the so-called Palestrina style. Through the secularization of life and music beginning in the sixteenth century and spreading in the seventeenth and eighteenth centuries, the legato moved from the center to the right wing of an area of expression that grew ever richer. The "sacred" legato becomes the "reflective" legato; it retains its original expression well for a long time in organ music, especially in that based on a cantus firmus; but already in the slow movements of the violin concertos and sonatas of Bach, still more in those of the Viennese Classical composers, it becomes increasingly the bearer of a subjective human feeling. To be sure, for the style of the great organ works of Bach a continuous legato is no longer taken for granted, and the adagio movements of the Viennese Classical composers are only rarely so expressive of suffering that they use legato exclusively for long periods of time — one must seek the adagio movements of the symphonies of Bruckner to luxuriate in legato. In three preludes to the music dramas of Richard Wagner the legato plays a significant role. It has an unearthly character in the high violins of the Prelude to *Lohengrin,* a sacred character in the Prelude to *Parsifal.* The Prelude to *Tristan and Isolde* must be regarded as the most inspired use of legato in the nineteenth century, for — with the exception of a pair of inhibiting *portato* sixteenth notes — from beginning to end it is kept in one single *legatissimo;* in order that it should describe "unquenchable longing, only once but in long, articulated sweep" the notes press together in narrow chromatic steps and intimate connections with one another.

THE STACCATO

The staccato has an area of expressiveness essentially broader than that of the legato, if one contrasts the conception of legato-connected music with all the shades of the almost limitless kinds of discontinuity. In staccato the conflict between individual note and melodic line comes into the open: instead of a single continuous line, we have to do with a punctuated one, between whose peaks we must establish the connection. The contrast of legato and staccato permits a comparison a) with the difference between quiet walking and hurried running, in which only the tips of the toes touch the ground, or   b) with the contrast between calmly collected behavior and excited gesture, such as the clapping of the hands, or   c) with the difference between thoughtful speech and emotional speech. All this must have become an ever more important area of expression in music the more music ceased to be a servant of the divine message, as it descended from heaven, spoke of human things to mankind, and learned to express in sound all the sorrow, all the blessedness of the human heart.

Positive as well as negative emotional states are richly served by staccato. Like the "la, la, la" refrains in the choral songs of the sixteenth century, there was in instrumental music too a "leggiero," which took everything lightly, danced and sprang, instead of walking. It is true that not until the Romantic period do we find continuous staccato (Weber, *Momento capriccioso,* Mendelssohn, *Scherzo in B minor*), but in the Viennese Classical period it played an ever greater role in the third and fourth movements of quartets and symphonies. High spirits can lead to persiflage, as in the second movement of Beethoven's Eighth Symphony, in which Mälzel is good-humoredly teased, or in the middle part of the Prelude to *Die Meistersinger* with the mocking of Beckmesser, or in *Ein Heldenleben* by Richard Strauss where he would make his opponent entirely ridiculous.

The staccato may serve as a transition to the negative side: the melody halts, it is afraid before the unguarded empty space over which it must travel. In the older literature, Handel made the most inspired use of this, in the musical depiction of "Mene tekel" in *Belshazzar,* where the violins unaccompanied have to play the following passage:

Characteristic examples from the works of Beethoven will be given in Chapter Eleven (Examples 133, 136, 137). As a fine example from the Romantic period, we may cite the end of the *Nachtstück* in C major by Schumann, in which we have the impression of uncertain steps losing themselves in the dark.

INTERMEDIATE GRADATIONS

Between legato and staccato are an endless number of intermediary steps, some of which musical practice has singled out and retained. The oldest and most important is the non-legato indicated by a combination of slur and dot. Through its very notation it discloses a conflicting area of feeling: the slur may remove or modify the separation, holding together what seeks to be separated. This is perhaps most movingly expressed at the close of the first movement of Beethoven's Sonata, Opus 111:

The strength of the *sforzando* attacks in the first two measures just barely allows the theme at the top of the chords (C-E♭-B) to be perceived; now the *sforzando* ceases, and along with the diminuendo the slur appears over the still dismembered melody, the separating force of the rests becomes gentler — it would be hard to find another example to compare in felicity of expression with this transition of only two measures, in which defiance is resolved into painful resignation.

Further examples of the non-legato will be given in the historical summary.

THE EFFECTS OF INTERVALS, OF NON-HARMONIC TONES, OF RHYTHM, OF PITCH AND INTENSITY UPON ARTICULATION

The smaller the intervallic distance between individual melody tones, the more easily the melody flows through them, with very little inhibition in diatonic scales and still less in chromatic scales. It is most natural to use legato in scalewise movement, but because it is so easily achieved, it has but little effect upon the expression. The greater the melodic tension becomes, whether it be through the dissonance of the intervals or through the size of the intervals, or through the two together, as in the beginning of the Adagio of Bruckner's Ninth Symphony,

the more the melodic line shows corners and peaks, the greater the danger that these corners and peaks may break through the legato — so much the greater is the expressive content if despite all this one is successful in keeping the line in a legato. Thus, especially in older music, where the course of the line is the primary thing, the most natural articulation is to bind together in legato the intervals of seconds, to separate slightly the notes of the middle-sized intervals by means of *portato*, and to separate distinctly the large intervals (those that we commonly designate as "leaps"). Several of the fugues of the *Well-Tempered Clavier*, for example the one in C major in Volume I, can be performed satisfactorily on the basis of these principles. The composer, however, need not follow the line of least resistance; he can draw a great deal more from deviations from the normal if he has the scale fly up in staccato, for example, as Mozart does so frequently in his piano sonatas and concertos, or, like Beethoven (as in the Rondo of the Sonata, Opus 2, No. 2), lets the chromatic scale rattle fortissimo. We have the opposite effect in the slurred tenths in Beethoven's Trio, Opus 1, No. 1, where one must stand on his toes in order to reach the interval, and the composer slyly lets the line fall down again brokenly:

The octave scale at the end of the G-minor Ballade of Chopin has the character of unleashed power.

If eighth notes are changed into sixteenths, for the most part leaps will become scale-steps, and the earlier staccato is changed thereby (and through the doubled rhythmic movement) to legato (Beethoven, String Quartet, Opus 18, No. 2):

As regards non-harmonic tones, what they all have in common is that whether they fall upon the accented or the unaccented beat, as dissonances they can claim no independent harmonic significance, and must resolve themselves a step higher or lower to their main note. Older music expressed both of these conditions clearly by notating non-harmonic tones in small notes and connecting them to the main notes with a little slur, which is never omitted, not even in otherwise unmarked music. Consequently for all neighboring tones, especially for the long and short suspensions, the linkage with the main note is to be taken for granted. There are exceptions to this rule only when between suspension and resolution a neighboring tone approached by a downward leap is inserted:

In this case the linkage may (but does not have to) be released in favor of the leap down. In Bach's motet *Jesu, meine Freude* the striking caesura is made more plausible through the comma in the text:

Only in later music does it more frequently happen that suspension and resolution are separated, as in Beethoven's Violin Sonata, Opus 12, No. 1, where, in addition, not the suspension but the resolution takes an accent in high-spirited mood:

It may at first glance seem surprising that the anticipation, which is an impatient preparation of the next note, is always tied to the preceding note:

(St. Matthew Passion)

The assumed basis for this conception, however, is that a legato progression in eighth notes underlies this progression. The release on the unaccented note strengthens the weight of the preceding main note; where there is no such release, as in the C♯-minor Waltz of Chopin:

the upbeat relationship is strengthened.

With respect to rhythm, just as a regular rhythm is suitable to the legato, so a jerky, broken rhythm (as the name already suggests) is suitable for the staccato. The best example for this is the Grave of

"French overtures," whose dotted rhythm (which reminded Goethe of the rapping of the staff of a master of ceremonies) is normally performed separated; in *Messiah* and in the *St. Matthew Passion* this interrupted rhythm is expressively related to depicting the flagellation of Christ. Here too deviations from the norm may achieve special effects, as in the connecting of the sixteenth back to the dotted eighth note, ♪. , a form which — as we shall see — has a special meaning in Bach.

In this context we must also discuss the upbeat. In older music it is normal for the upbeat to be separated from the note to which it leads, so that the accented part of the measure may thereby indirectly be given more weight. Almost no instance to the contrary may be found in the older music (except for linkages of two notes of an upbeat character), even where that music is otherwise marked throughout. Only with the Viennese Classical composers is the upbeat occasionally linked, if what follows immediately thereafter is separated, for which the Finale of Mozart's G-minor Symphony and the beginning of Beethoven's Sonata, Opus 10, No. 3 serve as well-known examples.

Pitch also affects articulation. The range from C to c^3, the range of the keyboard up to Bach's time, at the same time the total range of the four types of voices, the range within which the greater part of our present music also moves, represents the area of human habitation, above which the elves and other spirits tread their airy way (Berlioz's *Queen Mab*, Mendelssohn's *Midsummer Night's Dream*), below which the giants and the malevolent ones live (Wagner, *The Ring of the Nibelung*). Therefore the middle ranges are more suitable to the legato, the outer ones to the staccato. The same thing holds for tempo and for intensity. Only the organ is capable of a limitless legato even in the slowest tempo and in full play: almost no one can avoid noting the extraordinary effect of the Grave at the end of the middle movement of the Bach G-major Toccata. *Fortissimo* strengthens the individual meaning of the tone in contrast to the line; the most delicate pianissimo effect available to string players is achievable only in pizzicato. Inasmuch as the damping on our pianos stops at f^3, no legato above that note is possible;° only the violin can rise to the highest registers in legato (Beethoven, Violin Concerto, end of the first movement).

The secondary factors of musical articulation enumerated here, especially if they strengthen one another reciprocally, can occasionally exceed the primary ones in their effect and influence upon the total expressive content.

° On standard American Steinway pianos, the damping stops at $e\flat^3$. — Translator.

※≫ ※≫ ※≫ ※« ※« ※«

CHAPTER FIVE

Musical Articulation in the Seventeenth and Eighteenth Centuries

IT IS perfectly obvious that the various groups of instruments articulate in various ways. Since the plucked and percussion instruments are not capable of any linkage of notes, they remain outside of consideration here, leaving the three major categories of the wind instruments, the string instruments, and the keyboard instruments.

The wind instruments most nearly approximate the voice in their manner of producing sound; like the voice, they articulate through controlling or interrupting the flow of the breath. The flute responds especially easily and sensitively to it. Agricola (in his *Musica instrumentalis deutsch,* 1528) and Ganassi (in his *Fontegara,* 1535) deal with this subject; also Hotteterre, the flutist of Louis XIV, speaks (in his *Principes de la flûte,* 1707), very briefly to be sure, of the difference between *articuler* (to separate or articulate) and *couler* (to slur), where "two or more notes come from a single tongue impulse, which is designated by a slur over or underneath the notes." The importance of articulation for expression is first recognized by Quantz, who in his *Versuch einer Anweisung die Flöte traversiere zu spielen* (1752) demands that it should "animate the expression of passion in all pieces, magnificently or sadly, happily or pleasantly, or as one might wish." Despite all this, the flute, like all other wind instruments, had a lesser significance in the development of articulation, particularly in the seventeenth century, for by its very nature it remained far behind the stringed instruments in the range of its capacities to articulate.

Despite their great general musical utility, the keyboard instruments, too, remained for a long time in the background, for the manner of their articulation, through the striking and removing of the finger, permitted only a few variants (the use of the wrist in playing was discovered a good deal later, and the use of the arm later still); and articulation is less closely and naturally related to this instrument than to the winds. An accurate slurring was indeed early striven for, but was achieved late.

The lead in articulation fell of its own accord to the stringed instruments, especially to the violin, which presides over so great a realm of articulatory possibilities that Sevčik, in his Études, Opus 1, gives for one figure no fewer than 170 various rhythms, connections, and bowings in which it should be practiced.

In the sixteenth century, viol playing had reached a high point. For the most part the viol and the lute were taught together, as by Ganassi in his *Regola Rubertina* (1543); from this it becomes understandable (according to Alfred Einstein) that in viol playing too the bouncing bow was preferred. Ganassi had, in his two instructive works, founded a hair-splitting system of articulatory signs utilizing periods variously placed; it has not been carried further. In the seventeenth century still, as Leblanc reports, Marin Marais, chief gambist to Louis XIV, played in six various bowings, indeed, but "as poverty-struck in expression as a harpsichord. Like the ticking of a clock sounds this manner of playing with lifted bow, and the *tout en l'air*, which is so much like the strumming of a lute or guitar." The enthusiasts of the lute, whose "golden tone" Leblanc praises, were also the enthusiasts of the gamba with its delicate, fleeting tone; both instruments in the course of the seventeenth century fell more and more into the background compared to the more robust violin, which shortly seized the leadership for itself.

Mersenne sings the violin's praise in his *Harmonie universelle* (1636). He says of it that "it grips not only the ears and the intellect, but also the eyes; it touches, it delights, it overwhelms [*tangit, pascit, rapit*] and fills with an unspeakable pleasure, in a single word: along with this instrument's greatest simplicity, the greatest versatility is inclosed within it." Praetorius says in the *Syntagma musicum:* "The discant violin, the French *violon*, calls for beautiful passages, gracious accent, quiet long strokes, turns, trills, and so forth." The Italians preferred long bowstrokes, the French short bowstrokes; Germany lay in the middle between these two leading musical countries. Schütz complains in the

preface to the second part of his *Symphoniae Sacrae* (1647) that "the
steady, extended bowstroke on the violin is not yet known in practice
among us Germans." Corelli asked for this bowstroke in his Christmas
Concerto explicitly with the words *Arcate sostenute e come stà* ("with
long bowstrokes, and as it stands," i.e. without ornamentation). Of
the French style, Leblanc says that "in Lully's time ... the bowstrokes
were chopped off and a hatchet blow marked every measure or at least
every musical thought." As we learn from Andreas Moser, in 1683 a
concertmaster in Ansbach wished to leave his post because he could not
accustom himself to the "drills in the French manner" and did not wish
to participate in "this very short bowstroke." Entirely different from
the established French style, which was oriented toward accuracy and
discipline (we learn about it especially from Muffat's preface to the
second part of his *Florilegium musicum*), was the Italian style, which
depended upon a large, full, singing tone. "Here one no longer differentiates up- and down-bow. One hears continuous sound that is allowed
to swell and diminish like a singing voice ... thus entirely appropriate
to represent great passions" (Leblanc). This Italian style, for which
Corelli's Sonatas serve as the classic example, came to Paris too at the
beginning of the eighteenth century and prevailed there against the
"Lullists."

So long as playing was done with alternate bows, no bow-marking
was necessary; the degree of separation, from an almost imperceptible
change of bow to a heavy staccato, was left to oral teaching and the
taste of the player. Further, in particular the great virtuosi of the seventeenth century did not find it necessary to edit their own music; what
William Brade, Carlos Farina, Paul Westhoff, J. J. Walther, Biber, and
others may have got out of their instruments, we can only dimly guess
from the written copies of their works. Only when, about 1600, players
first began to take two or more notes on a single bow and indicated
this new technique with a slur over or under the note heads, was it
necessary to introduce special signs to indicate the separation of notes:
the wedge° (▼) and the dot (•). These new signs are introduced at
the same time as the numbers for the new technique of figured bass
and the symbols for Baroque ornaments. While we are relatively well-
informed about the early period of the figured bass notation, and the
symbols for ornamentation were quickly adopted, the beginnings of

° The German word *Keil* for this symbol does not have an exact English equivalent. In its earliest manifestations the sign was a small, vertical line over the note,
and this is the form in which it appears in many eighteenth-century manuscripts
and some prints. As time went on, however, engravers found it more convenient to
substitute a wedge-shaped sign (▼), and we are therefore using the term
"wedge" for *Keil* throughout this book. — Translator.

the markings for articulation are still obscure. At the outset the new signs found only a very limited distribution. They are limited — with a few exceptions — throughout the seventeenth century to the stringed instruments, especially the violin; clavier and organ music remained for a long time — until Bach — generally without markings, since one might rely upon an experienced musician to find and determine the articulation, as well as the tempo and registration, for himself. Even orchestra scores, especially of operas, remain generally without markings, in part from carelessness, for they were often written under great pressure and had to be ready at the beginning of the rehearsal period of a new season, in part because during the rehearsals the conductor-composer had time and opportunity enough to carry out his own intentions. Only at the beginning of the eighteenth century do the signs for articulation, together with those for tempo and dynamics, begin to appear regularly: but it is not until the Viennese Classical composers that we attain the degree of certainty in the markings in all these areas that we have since taken for granted. In the performance of older music, therefore, one must distinguish correctly from which half-century it comes; what is correct for the period of Philipp Emanuel Bach is not also automatically valid for Johann Sebastian Bach; what is suitable for J. S. Bach may not be for Corelli; what fits Corelli ought not be applied to Monteverdi without further investigation.

THE SLUR

The oldest and most important of the three signs, the slur, was already long in use as a tie between two like notes when, about 1600, its effectiveness was extended to indicate the close connection of two different notes, but at first only of two different notes separated from one another by the interval of a second. The use of the slur became established when the old ligatures, which had designated such a connection through a complex note figuration, became "unmodern" and gradually fell into disuse. Praetorius speaks of it in the *Syntagma musicum*: "*Omnes ligaturas intricates esse removendas ... et illarum loco hanc virgulam usurpandem esse*" ("all complicated ligatures should be removed and in their place this small slur should be placed," cited in Johannes Wolf, *Geschichte der Mensuralmusik*, I, page 391). This "curved line," the slur, was immediately understood symbolically: it lies as if protectively over the notes it connects, and it consequently invariably lies over the note heads, not over the tails or beams. How quickly this new technique spread abroad is shown by Scheidt's remark in his *Tabulatura Nova* of 1624, the largest collection of organ and clavier compositions of the time:

Where the notes are connected like this,   ♪♪♪♪ , it is a special kind [of playing], such as the violists are wont to do in sliding with the bow. For why should such a manner of playing by the most distinguished violists of the German nation not be usable, when it gives also to sweet-sounding organs, regals, harpsichords, and instruments [clavichords] a truly lovely and pleasant effect, on which account I have grown fond of this fashion of playing and have become accustomed to it.

From these lines it is to be understood that the new achievement also found quick entry into Germany, and that Scheidt, presupposing a light manner of playing, was able to transfer it to the keyboard instruments. The "lovely and pleasant" effect he praises in it, he makes use of with the almost naive joy of a discoverer when he provides a figure, which is first to be performed regularly, with little slurs in the repetition (DDT I, p. 151 and frequently elsewhere):

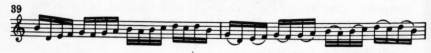

The requirements of playing as legato as possible on the keyboard instrument had already been raised in the sixteenth century, as when Diruta reproved organists, telling them they should press the keys, not strike them, stroke them, not slap them; bad organists he compared to the singer who takes a breath after every note. Against this, he permits the harpsichordists, when they play dances, to strike the instrument in order to make it speak more appealingly, and "in order to give the dances more gracefulness." Because the sound of the harpsichord dies away quickly, long notes must be struck several times (this holds true until Bach). The organ builder Antegnati demands (1608) of organists *"e si deve suonar adaggio con movimenti tardi e legato più che si può"* ("and one must play slowly with deliberate movements and as legato as possible"). When the Spanish monk Tomás de Sancta Maria, in his *Arte de tañer fantasia*, demands that in playing the ascending scale with the fingering 3 4 3 4 the performer should leave the third finger as long as possible upon the key "as though it were slid over the key," he means thereby the smoothest legato possible without using the thumb. Frescobaldi writes in his *Fiori musicali* (1635) that it is true that the Gregorian cantus firmi should properly be as

legato as possible, but to make performance easier *(per più commodità)*
might also be detached. Heinrich Albert, in the preface to the second
part of his *Arias* (1640), criticized the "chopping and thrashing" in the
playing of figured bass; Lorenzo di Penna demands, in his treatise on
the figured bass (1672), a legato playing *"che non si molesti la parte
cantante"* ("so as not to disturb the singer with a fancy accompaniment"); the French master of the organ, André Raison, wrote in 1687:
*"Le Grand Jeu se touche lentement et bien lier les Accords les uns aux
autres. La voix humaine se joue tendrement et bien lier."* ("The Great
Organ should be played slowly and the chords should be smoothly connected. The *vox humana* one should play delicately and very legato.")

The downbeat slurring of two melodically neighboring tones remained the most preferred articulation through Corelli to Bach. Note-
worthy in a Trio Sonata of Corelli is the change of mood with the
change of articulation:

Much bolder than Corelli and Legrenzi are the virtuosos of the
seventeenth century with whom slurring from upbeat to downbeat is
also no rarity, as in the Scherzi of J. J. Walther:

Indeed, the eccentric Carlo Farina in his *Capriccio stravagante* (1627)
exhibits a truly capricious alternation of both forms:

It is worth noting that two hundred years later, Paganini articulated in a similarly exciting fashion the following passage from Beethoven's Violin Concerto, which is unmarked in the original:

According to Moser, the Violinist Clement had played this passage in the same manner at the first performance of the Concerto, and Joachim, too, accepted this version for some time. Much rarer than in violin music are markings of this sort in music for clavier and organ; Scheidt's example found few followers. Two interesting exceptions may be cited here. The first is the end of Froberger's *Lament on the death of King Ferdinand IV,* a scale divided between the two hands, and joined together in groups of four beginning on the offbeat, a scale to be played quietly and delicately to the highest note of the clavichord, a scale upon which the soul of the king rises to heaven and is welcomed above by the lovingly sketched in heads of angels:

(In DTÖ VI, 2 the passage is in error, i.e. it is given as beginning on an accented note.)

The second example is found in a very free fugue by Hieronymus Pachelbel (the son):

(The quite unusual fingering, in the opinion of the editor of DTB II, 2, comes from a copyist.)

After 1700, the use of small slurs becomes more common, especially in the music of the French clavecinists, as in Couperin, who demands

of the player "a perfectly smooth connection" and who sometimes prefers to link every note to the next with a special little slur (*Pièces de
Clavecin*, Book II):

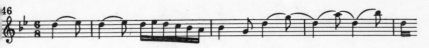

Rameau requires of the player a technically difficult separate articulation in each of the two hands in the first of his *Pièces de Clavecin en
concert:*

We are instructed on articulation in the music of the French Rococo
by a Father F. M. Engramelle in Paris, who constructed a mechanical
barrel organ with such precise instructions that one can infer from them
the desired tempo, as well as the performance of the ornaments and the
articulation. Hans-Peter Schmitz undertook this task. We conclude
from his treatise that Engramelle desired total legato only for long
suspensions, that in all other cases there should be a slight separation
between the notes. Apparently these remarkable instructions relate only
to the mechanical musical devices, and generalizations from them ought
not be made. Separated notes should be held longer in *Airs gracieux*
than in *Airs gais,* and shortest (for a quarter of their value) in the repetition of notes. These instructions as well ought not be transferred to
non-mechanical music without further examination.

REST, WEDGE, AND DOT

The most natural, and, before 1600, the only way to indicate the
separation of notes was with the rest. It served in older music not only
for phrasing, but also sometimes for articulation, especially in hocket-
like formations. In the *Ars nova* there also sometimes occur remarkable
interior rests, which Schering attributes to the fact that the part in
question was played by the organetto (the portative organ) and the

player needed the rests to fill the bellows with air again (Haas, p. 101). Occasionally, in order to indicate the rests with greater accuracy,

Rameau writes 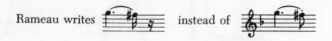 instead of

Beethoven, too, writes in his Quartet, Opus 95:

Because the rest expresses the isolation of the note more strongly than do articulation marks, it continued in use in this context in the Classical and Romantic periods. (Haydn, *Lark Quartet;* Beethoven, Fourth Symphony, first movement; Mendelssohn, Scherzo in B minor.)

Soon after 1600, however, the separation of notes is expressed through special symbols: the wedge and the dot. These are usually placed over (or under) the head of the note. If two new symbols are introduced at the same time, it is obvious that they were used with different meanings. That these two different meanings were not always observed in the period that immediately followed makes their consequent differentiation one of the most difficult and thankless jobs in the doubtful areas of old music. Both signs are first of all to be understood as belonging to the violin and its technique. The vertical wedge-shaped accent mark above the note isolates it and produces "a strongly concentrated and thereby especially accented sound, clearly separated from the adjacent tones, and produced with a short bowstroke, without forcing the tone" (Steglich). Indeed the wedge may stand as an accent sign over a group of notes, as in a concerto by Graupner (DDT 29/30, p. 204):

For the most part however, it stands over an individual note, which it shortens and accents at the same time.

The dot, which lengthens a note when placed alongside it, shortens it if placed over it, and at the same time takes away a part of its weight. To the "leggiero" in music, therefore, dots are more appropriate than wedges. The violinist can play this sort of staccato as well with a changing bow as on a single bowstroke, for there are available to him an almost limitless number of methods of bowing, for which expressions such as staccato, saltato *(sautillé)*, and others are common.

That the differentiation between the wedge and dot creates so many difficulties rests chiefly upon the happenstance that in many cases the engravers chose one or the other symbol not according to the composer's indication, but to suit their own convenience. It was perhaps out of resignation that an Italian composer, Manelli, in his Trio Sonatas, which appeared in 1682, left it to the engraver to choose which sign he should use (Moser, p. 69). The modern editor can carry out the distinction with certainty only where a work exists either in the marked manuscript of the composer, or in the engraved proof corrected by the composer himself, *and* if in these instances both symbols are used side by side. Of this there are several examples. From the *Pièces de Clavecin* of Couperin:

(The quarters are accented; the eighths are to be played lightly.)

Another instance is to be found at the beginning of Bach's D-minor Clavier Concerto:

In the finale of a symphony by Cannabich (of the Mannheim School) the accented parts of the measure take wedges; the remaining ones, dots:

Additional examples are given in the chapters on Bach, Mozart, and Beethoven (Examples 125-127, 133, 138, 141, and 142).

The increased sensitivity and attention brought to bear upon articulation at the beginning of the eighteenth century is demonstrated strikingly in the Concerto for Four Violins of Vivaldi (which Bach arranged for four harpsichords) in the following passage, whose glimmering charm consists exclusively of the varied bowstrokes of the four violins (one and three play staccato; two and four, legato in different patterns):

The contrast between legato and staccato is exploited more consciously, as in a violin cadenza by Heinichen (DDT 29/30):

together with the dynamic contrast between forte and piano. The period that followed also preferred this contrast: forte and staccato together versus piano and legato (Schobert, Mozart, see Example 124), while the older period (Biber) combines these elements differently: staccato, because less substantial, is joined with piano.

The extent to which notes are shortened is given variously by different authors. According to Muffat the shortening in duple meters is one half of the written value; in triple meters, one third. Couperin would shorten the sound on the quickly fading harpsichord only by a fourth, Quantz by one half. Philipp Emanuel Bach's statement is worth heeding: "One must make a distinction in staccato, and take into account the value of the note, whether it is half of a measure, a quarter, or an eighth, whether the tempo be swift or slow, whether the dynamic sense is forte or piano; these notes are always held for somewhat less than half their value. In general, it can be said that staccato takes place mostly with leaps and in fast tempo."

In this period, with Philipp Emanuel Bach and the North German lesser masters, the wedge was made narrower until it became a thin vertical stroke, which no longer bore a suggestive connotation. Since it could be confused with the number 1 for the thumb in the indication of fingering, Philipp Emanuel Bach preferred the dot. It is only shortly after 1800 that the wedge took on the significance of an especially sharp and short staccato (a quarter of the value of the note) in piano music, but its use is suppressed increasingly in favor of the dot, so that towards the end of the century it almost disappeared from the editions of Classical piano music in common use.

THE NON-LEGATO

The concept of the non-legato cannot be unequivocally defined, for in older music one ought not infer a non-legato manner of performance from the absence of any articulatory indication. Only in instances where slurs and dots are to be found can one assume that the unmarked passages should be played by the violinist with a change of bow, and the individual sounds be performed with a greater or lesser separation of the notes according to the character of the music. In the eighteenth century Marpurg still regards the non-legato as the normal articulation for the clavier: "Contrasted with legato as well as with staccato playing is the ordinary progression, in which one raises the finger from the preceding key quickly, shortly before striking a new key. Because this ordinary method is always assumed, it is never indicated." Philipp Emanuel Bach describes it in the following passage, from which it is to be concluded that he already assigned to the non-legato its own characteristic expressive value: "The notes that are neither staccato nor legato nor sustained are to be held for half their value, unless the abbreviation 'ten.' stands over them, in which case they must be held [to full value]. These notes are commonly the eighths and quarters in moderate and slow tempos, and must be played not weakly, but rather with a certain fire and an entirely light stroke." In place of the designation *ten. (tenuto)*, Türk later introduced the horizontal line over the note, which gives it a measured duration and accent; the Viennese Classical composers however did not yet use this new sign, which was adopted only in the course of the nineteenth century.

The non-legato indicated by a combination of slur and dots ⌢ has an entirely different expressive value. It is introduced into notation almost simultaneously with the wedge and dot as early as the seventeenth century. The violinist plays notes so designated without a change of bow, and with only a slight separation of the notes; in rapid tempo (flying staccato) he can, as compositions of J. J. Walther and others show, take 16 or more such notes on a single bow. Applied to the same note, this method of bowing produces the rhythmic tremolo, of which Monteverdi made use for the first time, as is well known, in his *Combattimento di Tancredi e Clorinda* (1624); he called this the "agitated style" *(stile concitato).* In slower tempos and in *piano* this method of bowing tends to be used for the expression of more delicate moods (Bach, *Christmas Oratorio*). Kuhnau makes use of it, carrying it over to the clavier, in his Biblical Sonatas for "The Trembling of the Israelites." In the period of the latest and highest development of the art of the clavichord, with Philipp Emanuel Bach, this designated non-legato receives a special significance. He writes of it. "The notes marked $\overset{\frown}{\cdots}$ are drawn out and each one equally receives a noticeable weight. The connection of notes through the slur with dots is called, in the case of the clavier, 'the carrying of the notes' " *(das Tragen der Töne).* Marpurg expresses himself similarly, and adds: "this can only be done on the clavichord, not on the harpsichord." (This "carrying of the notes" should not be confused with the *Bebung,* which on the clavichord would be designated through several dots and a single slur over *one* note.) Already with Couperin, but still more with Mozart, Beethoven, and in the music of the nineteenth century, the marked non-legato becomes a special area of expression, which lends delicacy, care, often also hesitation, indecision, and which already possesses an inconsistent notation (see Examples 3, 30, 93-96, 147, and 148).

With this is described the arsenal of symbols that were available to the Classical composers. Before there can be a discussion of their styles of articulation, however, it is necessary to speak of the construction of groups through articulation and of the relationship of slur and beam.

※≫ ※≫ ※≫ ≪※ ≪※ ≪※

The Construction of Groups
Through Articulation

AFTER HAVING considered phrasing and articulation in the last several chapters, as independent areas distinctly separated from one another, we now encounter one of the most interesting and the most controversial areas of musical grammar, that in which phrasing and articulation touch: the construction of groups through articulation. It is true that the theory of music has tried to draw a firm boundary between the two areas of our study, to designate the territory to the left as the province of phrasing and that to the right as the province of articulation; but this diplomatic action has in the main remained a paper decision because the Great Powers, namely the musicians, in their effective majority have not recognized it.

The problem is this: should the motivic figures that arise within a phrase through the connection of individual notes be reckoned as belonging to articulation or to phrasing? Should the violinist say, "I phrase this or that passage" or ought he say, "I articulate it"? Wiehmayer advocated the view that phrasing concerns only the phrase as a whole, and that motivic mergings within a phrase should not be designated with this name. The overwhelming majority of musicians however still tends to call such mergings "phrasing" too. Thus Rudolph Klein gives this definition: in the Austrian *Musikzeitschrift* (1950, Volume 5/6): "Phrasing is the thoughtful connection of a series of notes, comprising at least two notes ... the interruption of the melodic line is called articulation." It is however preferable to leave to the concept of phrasing its original clear meaning, and to designate the connection of two, three, or more notes, if they act in the formation of a motif, as "the construction of groups through articulation."

If a series of rising scale degrees

is given a single type of articulation (consistently legato or staccato) the sense of the connection of all the intervals remains unaffected. But if the rising thirds are slurred:

or the descending seconds:

new, opposing relations arise. In the first case, the falling seconds become "dead intervals" (Riemann), and in the second, the rising thirds are "dead." In Riemann's view one interpretation excludes the other; but it has been shown above that with such alternatives of articulation, violence is done to living music: these intervals are indeed weakened, but not "dead"; rather they are still available as complementary, and effective. With either an entirely legato or staccato performance, both rising thirds and falling seconds in Example 55 will be found to be equally strong, just as the rhythm ♩ ♫♩ ♫ taken by itself in isolation permits either a dactylic or an anapestic interpretation.

Because such connections can take on the meaning of a motif, it is necessary to demolish this notion of Riemann's, for in daily usage the concept of the "motif" is as ill-defined as that of the phrase. The well-known *Formenlehre* by Stöhr (newly revised edition by A. Orel and

H. Gál, 1950) defines it as follows: "By 'motif' is understood a succession of tones that achieves frequent repetition [!].... Such a succession of tones must be neither sharply defined nor especially striking rhythmically or melodically" (?). But Stöhr also calls one clearly set-off phrase, the theme of the first movement of the Sonata, Opus 2, No. 3 of Beethoven, a "motif"! We are better instructed by Riemann, who in his *Musiklexikon* (10th Edition) defines "motif" as a "compact segment of melody with a strong unity of expressive meaning." Kurth calls the motif the "smallest complete melodic unit," Grabner understands by it "the smallest autonomous melodic segments," Wiehmayer, "the smallest organic elements of the tonal language." Worthy of note is a remark of Mattheson, who in his *Das neu-eröffnete Orchestre* (1713) says that "the smallest motifs, like the adverbs in language, often have the greatest strength." The strongest element in the merging of tones into a motif is rhythm; there are, however, especially in older music, and particularly in J. S. Bach, instances in which the regularly moving rhythm presents no stopping-place, and the course of the melodic line permits several meanings. In such a case a composer — or if he has not done it, the interpreter — can create groups of notes with the significance of motifs through articulation.

Here again one must take exception to the *Phrasierungslehre (Grammar of Phrasing)* of Hugo Riemann and the *Phrasierungsausgaben (Phrased Editions)* which that great pioneer and scholar issued about 1890, and through which he raised a huge confusion of concepts whose aftereffects are noticeable even today. At that time he was a piano teacher in Hamburg, and "he took pity on the people" for the soulless, mechanical piano-playing of musicians as well as of amateurs. He tried to revive for them a feeling for the living powers of music, especially through the upbeat interpretation of motifs: "The upbeat is to man a primary and inborn basic hereditary law"; "In the beginning was the upbeat." He tried to make this "upbeatness" recognizable in the printed music, notably sometimes against the intention of the composer. Thus, for example, he described the downbeat version (a) of Beethoven's Sonata, Opus 7 as "lame," and the version he constructed (b) as "boldly leaping up";

It was however precisely the descending third that Beethoven made the principal motif of the entire first movement. The final theme of a Mannheim symphony

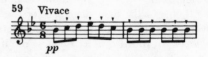

Riemann interpreted as follows:

In the subject of Bach's D-minor Clavier Concerto (see Example 51) he altered the meter and the beams, and suppressed the original articulation.

Examples of this sort could be multiplied at will; they naturally excited powerful opposition among colleagues, except for a small, fanatic following: the *Phrased Editions* which had not been well received anyway because they were difficult to read, soon disappeared from the market. Riemann had furthermore seen the necessity of improving his teaching, and worked at it up until his death. He must have felt frustrated, because he sought to do the impossible; he tore the exterior surface off music, in order to be better able to show the interior. He underrated the esthetic laws peculiar to articulation as well as its power to build motifs; he gave the following definition: "Articulation is primarily something mechanical, technical; phrasing primarily something ideal, perceptional. I articulate well in the following theme:

(Brahms, Second Symphony) if I connect the slurred notes to one another and disconnect distinctly the last note under this slur; I phrase well if I understand that here this last note, together with the first under a new slur, creates a motif":

What a contradiction in itself! The first version I should perform because it is written that way; the second I should "understand" but not perform because it is not so written! In the Brahms theme, which moreover reads in full as follows:

in the absence of any sort of designation, on rhythmic as on harmonic grounds the last quarter would connect more easily with the note that follows it than with the note that precedes it; the composer however has explicitly demanded this slurring with the preceding notes; thus there can be no doubt that the motif is not, as Riemann would have it,

♩ | ♩   but | ♩   ♩ | The upbeat reading would introduce too

much activity into this beginning, which is intended to be quiet and pensive. This could have been achieved also through a legato slur spanning the four measures, but it is not within the capability of the horns to play the whole phrase in this manner, and beyond that — and this is the more important reason — through the slurs there arises a charming symmetry between measures one and four and between measures two and three. A glance at the treatment of both motifs in the development section removes completely any further possible doubt. It would be ridiculous to do battle with a dead lion, but Riemann's *Phrasierungslehre* has had a long-lasting effect; we shall encounter it again in the concluding part of this book in speaking of the editions of Classical organ and piano works that appeared shortly before 1914 and remain in use today.

Theodor Wiehmayer, in his *Musikalische Rhythmik und Metrik (Musical Rhythm and Meter)*, has done the service of setting right the state of affairs that Riemann set askew. But he too undervalues articulation when he sees in it only a "decorative garb with which the composer covers his thought." Rather one might say that articulation is the skin that lies protectively over the wonderful organism of the musical work of art, permits all its functions to be observed without laying them bare, and in its healthy circulation and tension brings the beauty of the musical substance to expression. There is in music nothing that is merely superficial; there are only functions of the musical organism some of which are more apparent from without, and some that remain more hidden in the interior.

SLUR AND BEAM

Riemann's ideas of reform were strongly influenced by the fact that in older as in Classical music, the end of a slur in many instances does not coincide with the end of a motif or a phrase, but the slur for the most part ends with the beam and is very rarely carried over a barline. Was it not better, in such cases, instead of several small, apparently illogically applied slurs, to draw one single large phrasing slur, and to carry it to the very last note of the phrase or motif?

In fact this problem belongs, like "wedge or dot?", to the most difficult specific questions that face us here. Until the middle of the eighteenth century, slurs that extended beyond a beam or across a barline were extremely rare (see one instance in Example 46); from then on they become more numerous, although they still remain exceptions. Only in the nineteenth century do continuous slurs occur more frequently, especially in piano music; but even there markings are to be found that appear to us incomprehensible and wrong, as in Mendelssohn's Second Organ Sonata,

where surely at least the first three measures are to be drawn together under one slur.

We must therefore try to distinguish between the instances in which such slurs were drawn simply as a matter of convenience, especially of the engraver (as in the distinction between the wedge and the dot), and those in which the composers demanded a change of bow from the string players and carried over this designation to the keyboard instruments as well.

The first instance is especially frequent in older music. Thus in the Bach organ chorale *Ich ruf zu dir, Herr Jesu Christ* the slurs over every quarter beat in the autograph score are to be understood as a continuous legato:

Similarly, it would be senseless in the first measure of Beethoven's G-major Rondo to make a break after the trill because the slur ends there:

Every player will easily find similar examples for himself. However, it is not true, as so many editors believed about 1900, that one should simply lengthen every slur that appears peculiar or illogical at first sight; rather the player, especially the pianist, must sharpen his sense for the nuances of the marking if he does not immediately understand it. If the slur ends just before the final note of a phrase, that note receives thereby a scarcely perceptible accent, as in the theme of Mozart's D-major Rondo:

Notes may be separated more markedly if it is a question of a suspension, as in the Sonata (K. 311):

Similarly there may be a good reason when, as at the beginning of the
F-major Sonata (K. Anh. 135), the slur ends before the beginning of a
measure, which is thereby accented:

Where Mozart carries the slur over, as in the *Jupiter Symphony*,

the last note dies away. Also interesting is the comparison of the articulation of the C-minor Fugue as Mozart first set it for two pianos, and as
he later arranged it for string quartet; in the later version the articulation was moderated:

Comparison of the theme and the first variation of the Variations in
F major is instructive too:

Rapid upbeat notes are sometimes notated thus:

sometimes thus:

The pianist who wishes to differentiate the two types can do it with the help of the given fingerings. There will be found, however, even with the most careful comparison of all sources, a large number of cases in which only the "feel" of the fingertips can decide. That, in several of the examples cited, the editors (earlier and later) have changed the original markings according with their own judgment has been noted here; all of the "popular" or "teaching" editions that appeared about or before 1900 are highly suspect.

The first person who contributed decisively to an improvement was Heinrich Schenker. He says, in the preface to his edition of Beethoven's Piano Sonatas: "The deeply meaningful play of beams: they announce to the eye the intent for belonging together here, for separation there. The secret eloquence of the slurs: now they draw what belongs together to a unity or emphasize its parts, now they expressly contradict a relationship, in order to intensify the need for it; often they appear simultaneously in different lengths with contradictory effects." Whoever plays Classical music must declaim it like a poem: a good reciter will take care not to concern himself primarily with clarifying the sense of the poem to the hearer, he assumes that the hearer will grasp that by himself; the reciter's principal aim will be to convey the more subtle and more hidden expressive values. Similarly, in music the primitive comprehension of a melody is to be presumed, and the player concerns himself with the subtle and hidden expressive values; for these, music places the most diverse means at his disposal, including both slur and beam in their manifold relationships.

PART TWO

※ ≫ ※ ≪ ≪ ≪

Phrasing and Articulation in the Works of Bach, Mozart, and Beethoven

In the second part of this treatise the basic principles and concepts established in the first part will be applied to the individual styles of the great masters, in particular to Bach, Mozart, and Beethoven. Each of the three masters has his own strongly delineated style in phrasing and in articulation. If Bach is here treated with special thoroughness, that is because recognition of the proper phrasing is more difficult with him than it is with the Viennese Classical composers, and because the question of intelligent articulation is of greater significance in practice, especially in his clavier and organ works. The overwhelming majority of his works is not marked and it is therefore necessary to draw conclusions for the unmarked works from those that are marked, and to apply similar principles to provide the missing signs of articulation. The most varied attempts to solve this problem have been made for more than a hundred years, but it is only in recent decades that we have begun to come close to a true solution. Mozart and Beethoven, on the other hand, expressed their intent with such clarity — Mozart with fair consistency, Beethoven invariably — that nothing further is necessary than to obey it. To obey it, however, one must know it, and there stood in the way until recently falsifications of articulation in many widely used editions dating from the turn of the century, indeed sometimes even in the critical Collected Editions of these masters. Today we are in the fortunate position of possessing pure *Urtext* editions of a number of Classical works; still greater is the number of editions in which the original and the editor's version are separated from one another with sufficient clarity.

⋙ ⋙ ⋙ ⋘ ⋘ ⋘

Phrasing in the Music of Johann Sebastian Bach

THE DISTINCTION established at the outset between musical prose and poetry is of especial significance in Bach, for the proportion of prose works (fugues, preludes, toccatas, and so forth) is greater with him than it is with the Viennese Classical composers. Stemming from poetry, hence from song and dance, in Bach's instrumental music are primarily those movements of his suites that are still purely dance-like in character — the minuet, gavotte, bourrée, passepied, and the much older sarabande. These are all regularly built from two- or four-measure units; a rare exception is the gavotte from the third English Suite, of which the second part begins with six instead of four half measures. Consequently, in movements of this type no explicit indication of the phrasing is necessary.

In the simple chorale movements with which the cantatas end, Bach indicated the phrasing, that is the end of every line, by means of the recently introduced fermata (see page 16). The question whether the fermatas here are only to be taken as reading signs, or whether one must pause on them, has been much discussed. The real reason for the fermata in the chorale — to give the congregation time to take a breath — disappeared in concert performances of the cantatas and Passions. Where Bach wished to have a large caesura — in the final chorale of Cantata 140, *Gloria sei dir gesungen* — he used rests in addition to the fermata; in the *Orgelbüchlein* and in other little organ chorales, similarly, there are fermatas at the end of every line, although, because of the motion in the remaining voices, it would be impossible to hold them (in the large fantasies on the chorale, in which the segments of the chorale melody are separated by rests, there are no fermatas). These fermatas, therefore, are only reading signs, they serve for easier comprehension, and a conductor who wishes to sustain them in the chorales cannot justify this practice by the notation. As regards fermatas at the end of instrumental movements, Bach distinguishes clearly between the fermata on the final note and that on the double bar after the final note — in the latter case the music should continue to sound inaudibly in the mind, without prolongation of the final chord.

Between poetry and prose are those forms that still show the regularity of poetry but are already permeated with the prose elements of counterpoint; examples of this are the chorales of the *Orgelbüchlein*, the Passacaglia for organ and the Chaconne for violin, and further, those movements whose theme is regularly constructed ($2 + 2 = 4$ measures), like the first movement of the *Italian Concerto*, the fifth and sixth Partitas for clavier, and the Eb-major Prelude for organ (the development of which, however, quickly abandons this regularity). The allemandes and gigues (in part also the courantes), retaining little of their dance character, approach still nearer to prose. Their two sections consist of a number of measures almost always regularly divisible by four (12, 16, 20, and so forth) but within each section they cannot be regularly divided further. Only a few musicians will be in a position to recognize this regularity in the larger sense despite the irregularity in the smaller. The phrasing of the allemande is therefore no longer comparable to that of verse, but derives from prose — that is, it is to be determined from the logical delineation of the motives and phrases.

That the polyphonic style is entirely to be derived from prose was established at the outset. In the late period of this style, however, in the case of Bach, there are themes that are constructed with strophe-like regularity. Among these are fugue subjects consisting of several phrases each, for example in the C-minor, Eb-major, F-major, G-major, G-minor, B-major fugues of the first book of the *Well-Tempered Clavier*; and among the organ works, the subjects of the fugues in A major (Peters Vol. II, 3), G minor (II, 4), C major (III, 8), E minor (III, 10), C minor (IV, 5), G minor (IV, 7), and others. The great popularity of the C-minor Fugue for clavier and the two G-minor Fugues for organ can be attributed at least partly to the regular structure of their subjects; the C-minor Fugue with $2 + 2 + 4$ beats; the "Great" G-minor Fugue, $4 (2 + 2) + 4 + 4$; the "Little" G-minor Fugue $8 + 4 + 8$ beats. Fugues developed throughout from this sort of subject are easier to grasp than fugues on pure prose themes.

Bach himself gives important hints about how to phrase his large in-strumental works in the compositions for two manuals, when, in the course of a movement, a voice shifts from one manual to another. From these transfers we can see how Bach himself phrased. Examples occur in the *Italian Concerto,* the first and last movements of the *French Over-ture* (or Partita in B minor) from the second part of the *Klavierübung,* and in the following organ works: Organ Concerto in D minor after Vivaldi, the "Dorian" Toccata (III, 3), the Organ Concertos in G minor, A minor, and C major (VIII, 1, 2, and 4; the latter, to be sure, handed down only in copies).

In harpsichord music, the two manuals are indicated by the words "forte" and "piano"; in organ music they are indicated by "O. W." (*Ober-werk*) and "R. P." (*Rückpositiv*). The four parts of the *Klavierübung* have been published in an *Urtext* edition by Peters (edited by Soldan), as have the *Brandenburg Concertos* (Soldan), the *English Suites* (Kreutz), the Inventions and the *Musical Offering* (Landshoff); the *Well-Tem-pered Clavier* has been available for nearly a hundred years (Kroll); Bärenreiter has published the Sonatas for Violin with obbligato harpsi-chord and for Flute with obbligato harpsichord; the Sonatas and Parti-tas for Unaccompanied Violin and the Suites for Unaccompanied Cello exist in several editions (the Violin Sonatas also in a facsimile edition). For the organ works, Griepenkerl's edition published by Peters (a new edition revised by me) may be regarded as an *Urtext*; as is well known, a new Complete Edition of the works of Bach published by Bärenreiter is under way.

In the *Italian Concerto* we see — in addition to the transfers of manual made clear by the use of rests — in almost every passage an upbeat transfer of manual frequently emphasized by breaking the beam, as in the first movement:

In only one case (measure 129) does the transfer of manual fall on the accented part of the measure, in order not to impair the melodic character of the descending fifth:

In the third movement, the word "forte" is placed in the original at the transfer of manual in the right-hand part in measures 29, 49, and 171, and in the left-hand part in measures 33, 53, and 175 in such a fashion that it is not clear whether it refers to the first or the second quarter note; the transfer of manual is more musical if the right hand changes on the second quarter and the left hand on the first quarter.

In the *French Overture,* the transfer that takes place successively in all voices from subsidiary theme to main theme in measures 89 to 95 is worth noting and is of importance, for it can serve organists as a model for many similar cases in the organ fugues:

Of the organ works, the "Dorian" Toccata in particular — even though
its autograph has not survived — shows so intelligent and often bold a
change of manual that it could only stem from Bach himself. Especially
striking is the rapid transfer, after each pair of eighth notes in measures
31 through 33; Bach may have borrowed this device from French organ
music. In this Toccata, the important thematic transfers of manual are
made on the first beat of the measure, while in the Weimar concerto
transcriptions they are almost always made on the offbeat,

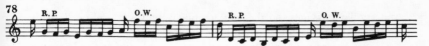

indeed even at the expense of the main theme, as in the Concerto in
G major:

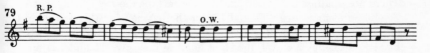

Anyone who would phrase (but not articulate) the great majority of
the unmarked works of Bach in the style of these examples should guard
against that mistake most frequently made by beginners: to use too
marked a separation. Not every phrase-ending obligates us to make the
end as clear as possible to the listener; to treat it so can easily create a
fatally pedantic impression. Nor should the end of a fugue subject be
separated from what follows, since in some cases the point of termina-
tion cannot be determined with certainty, as in the first fugue of the
Well-Tempered Clavier; in other cases the subject is so closely linked
with the continuation that no caesura may be introduced, as in the subject of the *Art of the Fugue*:

One should also take care not to detract from Bach's great melodic
line, which consists chiefly of development in a chain of phrases, by
breaking down the sequence too obviously into its members. The first
Two-Part Invention may serve as an example. Since the piece is generally familiar, there is no need to reprint it here; to follow our discussion,
it is suggested that the reader have the music at hand.

The wonderful consistency with which Bach developed this entire piece from a single idea can mislead us into attempting to make this motive easily recognizable everywhere, especially in the sequence in measures 3 and 4:

and similar passages; on the modern piano, however, only a light dynamic shading, at most, should be applied to the bracketed figure. Larger caesuras not indicated by rests are found only at the beginning of measures 15 and 19. In the sequences in measures 15 through 18, one ought not make a separation in every half measure, but should connect the top voice in measures 16 and 18 because of the suspensions. There are small, scarcely perceptible caesuras for the right hand at the beginning of measures 2, 3, and 13; for the left hand at the beginning of measures 3, 5, 8, 9, 10, and 11; other still smaller caesuras (the left hand in measures 3 and 4; the right hand in measures 11 and 12) are all already sufficiently clarified through the larger interval, hence require no further interruption.

Reference was made at the beginning to the difficulty of a meaningful phrasing in the fugues. It arises from the fact that almost never do all voices reach a point of rest at the same moment, and that while each voice should be treated independently, all together are subject to the higher law of harmonic polyphony. Their independence is thus not unlimited, and because of the "monarchic orientation of our consciousness" (Groos) it is scarcely possible for us to give an equal amount of attention at the same moment to all four voices of a fugue. A fugue is a multi-leveled structure: each new thematic entry seeks to draw attention to itself and this, especially in stretti, often leads to a state of suspense from which only the subsequent cadence leads us back to solid ground. Nor does the composer treat all voices as of equal value; while non-thematic inner voices need never be degraded to mere fillers, Bach's own fugues offer examples enough wherein they are given less independence than the leading voices. Anyone who wishes to phrase the first fugue of the *Well-Tempered Clavier* will find that all the necessary phrase divisions are made self-evident, since the entry of the theme is prepared by rests; the few instances in which there is no rest (as in measure 14), also permit no separation. Through the clear setting off of its subject and its two countersubjects, the second fugue, too, also offers no difficulties of phrasing.

Of the organ fugues, the well-known "Great" Fugue in G minor may serve as an example. Its unremittingly moving sixteenths must be subdivided, for example the continuation of the subject in the pedal in measure 57 ff.:

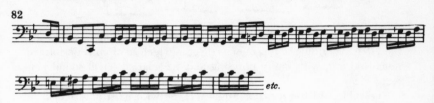

similarly the corresponding passage in the soprano (measure 97 ff.):

In the places marked with a small stroke, there is no opportunity to "take a breath"; nor should the preceding note be shortened, because it would thereby lose its weight. The only remaining method is to play the three sixteenths that follow the stroke leggiero in order to make them recognizable as a light upbeat:

The motif-grouping in measures 39 through 41 will be heard only if the two voices are phrased independently:

similarly in the final measures:

If it is phrased in this fashion and articulated intelligently (see Example 118), everything in this famous piece — which so often is performed much too fast, with faulty phrasing and articulation — will sound perfectly clear.

The subject of the A-major Fugue (II, 3) with its structure of 2 + 2 + 5 measures, must be both phrased and articulated as follows:

The counter rhythm │ 𝅗𝅥 𝅗𝅥 │ will be understood only if the quarter note is detached slightly, otherwise the subject would be heard as follows:

Both types of detaching — the one for the phrasing, the other for the articulation — will be performed by the player in the same fashion, for the organ permits no nuances; they must, however, be understood completely differently by the listener. Perhaps this is the real reason why this fugue has assumed a special place among the organ fugues of Bach and is not felt to be truly "organistic."

※ ※ ※ ※ ※ ※

CHAPTER EIGHT

The Articulation of the Bach Chamber Music

THE STYLE of articulation of the figured bass period found its final, richest expression in the works of Bach. Just as this master rose above all his predecessors and contemporaries in greatness of conception, in mastery of all the elements of composition, in inspiration even in the smallest forms, so his style of articulation was bolder — as well as more thoroughly thought out — than that of any other composer of his time; it was not until Mozart and Beethoven that equal heights were attained.

The tendency of the late Baroque to slur together small groups of notes ruled the style of Bach as well. Continuous slurrings are rare with him; there are only a few cases so marked (more frequently in the later than in the early works); a continuous staccato, too, appears only occasionally, and then chiefly in the bass. To be sure, it is not always easy to discern the composer's intention from the autograph copy, for Bach frequently places his slurs so high over the notes that it is not clear whether they should be valid for all four sixteenths of a quarter or only for three, and for which three.

The largest number and the most characteristic markings we find in the cantatas, especially in the obbligato instrumental parts to arias, which are often marked with painstaking precision. In second place are the chamber works (especially those for small groups); in last place are the works for clavier and organ, which, with few exceptions, are unmarked. Anyone who wishes to mark these works cannot merely content himself with completing the few given markings, but must make comparisons with the cantata parts and the chamber music; and he can do this more readily because in Bach's tonal language there is a stronger unity in this area than in that of the keyboard instruments, where he is more concerned with an idiomatic style. Therefore, in these works, the markings, where they are to be found, are to be understood in the style and idiom of the stringed instruments.

The first Bach scholar to investigate this area and concern himself about its meaning was Albert Schweitzer; for a long time he remained the only one. It is surprising how little space in the enormously expanded Bach literature of recent decades is given to so extraordinarily important a matter. In his *J. S. Bach,* whose epoch-making significance was recognized more by amateur than by professional musicians, Schweitzer dedicated no fewer than forty pages to this question, and opened the eyes of the reader through numerous musical examples. It is true that we will seek the word "articulation" there in vain; he thought of articulation, as was generally the practice about 1900, within the concept of phrasing. Schweitzer was especially taken with the cantatas. "Whoever has attentively studied these works, or some of them, feels himself transported into an entirely new world of note succession. A wealth of tonal combinations that were previously undreamed of is disclosed. The most wonderful thing about it, however, is that this multiplicity manifests itself not as a multiplicity of accident or caprice, but seems to have sprung from the treatment of certain basic ideas as to the combination of a complex of notes into a long musical period." (What is meant is the articulation of groups.) Unfortunately some of Schweitzer's own suggestions for "phrasing" fugue subjects from the *Well-Tempered Clavier* are in irreconcilable contradiction to this penetration into the style. They were obviously influenced by Riemann — for example, when the subject of the F-minor Fugue from the first book is marked in the following fashion:

89

In recent decades Schweitzer has undertaken no further revision of his work. Despite the extraordinary advance of Bach scholarship, Schweitzer's work still has its applicability — with the exception of those sections derived from Riemann, which one would gladly see altered or excised.

LEGATO

Because of its descriptiveness the continuous legato, chiefly made up from smaller slurs, is generally closely associated in Bach with the imagery of the movement of waves, as in the Crucifixion Cantata (No. 56, in the recitative "Mein Wandel auf der Welt ist einer Schiffahrt gleich") in the figure of the obbligato cello:

Similarly in a number of other cantatas, such as No. 88 (*Siehe, ich will viel Fischer aussenden*), No. 26 (in the aria "So schnell ein rauschend Wasser schiesst"), and No. 178 ("Gleich wie die wilden Meereswellen"). In the solo cantata *Weichet nur, betrübte Schatten* (No. 202), the slurs lie like veils over the drawn-out figures of the violin. For the most part, however, Bach conceives a legato as a sign of mourning, of tranquil sorrow, as at the beginning of Cantata 46 (*Schauet doch und sehet*), in Cantata 21 ("Seufzer, Tränen, Kummer, Not"), Cantata 85 ("Seht, was die Liebe tut"), the introductory Sinfonia to Cantata 12 (*Weinen, Klagen*). On several occasions, "piano" is expressively added to legato, from which one should infer the delicate execution of the legato in performing the slow movements of the chamber music, of the Trio Sonatas for organ, and the *Italian Concerto* (see also Example 65).

STACCATO

Bach rarely writes a continuous staccato; when he does, he uses it especially in the bass, when the attention should be entirely directed to the melodic voices, as in a number of cantata arias (Cantatas 1, 2, 6, 8, 20, and many others). In the chamber music it achieves its most beautiful effect in the bass, to be performed quasi-pizzicato, over which the two canonic upper voices play in the third movement of the A-major Violin Sonata:

As a means of expression, Bach does not use the staccato with the freedom later employed by Mozart and Beethoven, but he does use it in various ways for tone-painting: bitingly in Cantata 181 ("Der schädlichen Dornen unendliche Zahl"), roughly in Cantata 102, where even the choral voices are marked staccato ("Du schlägest sie, aber sie fühlen es nicht"):

brusquely in the Cantata *Herkules am Scheidewege* (No. 213), where the hero rejects the blandishments of sensual pleasure ("Ich will dich nicht hören"). It is characteristic that this "staccato sempre" is lacking in the parody of this aria in the *Christmas Oratorio* ("Bereite dich, Zion") just as it is lacking in the G-minor Mass, where the movement from Cantata 102 was used once more. In the *St. Matthew Passion* ("Buss and Reu"), the notes of the two flutes fall softly like "the drops of my tears." The lightly winged staccato is seldom found in Bach (No. 181, *Leichtgesinnte Flattergeister*). He differentiates between the wedge and dot in only a few instances and only in his late works (see Example 51). It is strange that the solo works for violin and cello show almost no staccato marks at all.

NON-LEGATO

Bach uses the non-legato, expressed by dots with slurs, in various ways, but always in delicate shadings. In Cantata 61 ("Siehe, ich stehe vor der Tür und klopfe an") the knocking is depicted not only by the string orchestra, which accompanies in pizzicato, but also by the solo voice:

In the *St. Matthew Passion* ("Und da sie den Lobgesang gesprochen hatten, gingen sie hinaus an den Ölberg") the basses symbolize timid hesitation before the impending scene of suffering:

In Cantata 30, where the "cry of the Saviour" echoes:

the articulation prevents the notes in the echo from being obliterated. Dots with slurs are rare in the chamber music, as in the E-major Violin Sonata, in a manuscript copy that may well be counted as authentic:

Where unmarked passages occur in otherwise marked works, Bach requires non-legato, that is, a change of bow after every note, but with little separation. Not all unmarked parts, however, should be performed in this fashion, for often, especially in the bass parts of the church works, the articulation signs are omitted only because of haste. Here again Schweitzer was the first to make us aware how barbaric it was to scrape all the unmarked bass parts to the arias in a wooden non-legato. He noted, correctly, that in many instances the effect of an aria can depend upon the lively or dull articulation of the basses. For grand, festive movements, such as the Gloria of a Mass, the grand *détaché* of the strings is of course the preferred bowing, because it is the one with which they can achieve the greatest brilliance.

THE ARTICULATION OF GROUPS

The simplest and oldest form of articulation of groups, the downbeat connection of two notes, still plays an important part in Bach (but no

longer in Mozart). It is obviously always found in the resolution of
suspensions, as in the subject of the B-minor Fugue from the first book
of the *Well-Tempered Clavier,* in Cantata 140 ("Zion hört die Wächter
singen"):

97

(similarly in the organ version of this movement, Peters VII, 57), and
with anticipations (the final chorus of the first part of the *St. Matthew
Passion*) which, especially when rising upward, are frequently interpreted as "sobs" (*O Lamm Gottes unschuldig* in the *Orgelbüchlein,* the
lament in the *Capriccio on the Departure of His Beloved Brother*); in
Cantata 20 ("Ewigkeit, du machst mir bange") even in the vocal part:

98

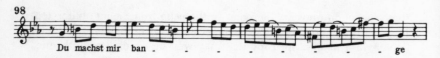

Beyond these, however, Bach makes use of this grouping almost as a
formula, in order to express submission to the will of God, peace, and
security. Here are a few among many examples: Cantata 159 ("Es ist
vollbracht"), where the slurring also occurs in notes that are twice as
long in the bass; in the Gloria of the B-minor Mass ("Et in terra pax");
in the *St. Matthew Passion* ("Geduld, wenn scharfe Zungen stechen"),
where articulation and rhythm express the contrast between patience
and sharp-tongued attack almost too realistically:

99

In the Last Supper scene of the Passion, this group-form enters only
with the words "Ich werde von nun an nicht mehr von diesem Gewächs
des Weinstocks trinken bis an den Tag, da ich's neu trinken werde mit
euch in meines Vaters Reich" ("From now on I will drink no more of
the fruit of the vine until that day when I shall drink anew with you in
my Father's kingdom"). It is even more meaningful in Cantata 89
(Was soll ich aus dir machen, Ephraim?) and Cantata 40 ("Die

Schlange, so im Paradies") where the music contributes the comfort the text withholds.

Bach also loved this form in chamber music, and it enhances the beauty of many slow movements. Its use is striking in the *Double* of the Allemande of the B-minor Suite for Unaccompanied Violin, which it rules almost exclusively. In Cantata 22, it is reserved to the strings, while the oboe articulates thus ♫♫♫ ; similarly it appears in the third movement of the Gamba Sonata in G major with obbligato harpsichord.

In its triplet interpretation, ♩♪₃ , the pattern of dotted eighth and sixteenth appears almost always in the Baroque in pastoral movements, from the Pastorale of Corelli's *Christmas Concerto,* to Handel's *Messiah* and the shepherd's music in Bach's *Christmas Oratorio.* The third movement of the Violin Sonata in C minor is also to be performed as a triplet, with a gentle subjective expression:

The tense punctuated rhythm ♩.♩ became especially meaning-ful for Bach; Schweitzer hoped "that the existence, the significance, and performance of this rhythm in Bach might one day be made the subject of a thorough study." In contrast to the continuously disconnected punctuated rhythm of the French overture, the slurring back of the sixteenth to the preceding dotted eighth gives this "rhythm of solemnity" warmth and animation and at the same time an ·inner tension that has found its noblest expression in the E♭-major Prelude for organ (which in itself prohibits too fast a tempo for this famous, often incorrectly performed piece):

The introductory Adagio of the C-major Sonata for Unaccompanied Violin conveys an almost other-wordly far-away expression:

The upbeat form occurs more rarely. It is introduced with the expression of an urgent plea in Cantata 11 ("Ach bleibe doch, mein liebstes Leben"):

Bach used this aria again in the Agnus Dei of the B-minor Mass: what was longing in the Cantata is now interpreted as sorrow; Bach, in addition, constructs in the melody of the alto voice the shape of the cross:

(if one connects the first and fourth and the second and third eighth notes, a cross lying on its side is drawn); and the solemn form of the figure, ♩♩♩♩ appearing by contrast in the ritornello, expresses submission to the will of God — an example of the manifold character of Bach's tonal language.

GROUPS OF THREE

Groups of three in sixteenth-note movement are introduced either as

or as   Both forms are charmingly combined in

the *Christmas Oratorio:*

Frequently three slurred notes stand at the beginning of the measure
to strengthen the natural accent of the measure (Violin Sonata in E
major):

still more frequently however they wander through the measure, as in
the Minuet of the E-major Suite for Unaccompanied Violin, where, as
a result of a cross-rhythm, the following results:

The solo sonatas and suites for violin and cello naturally show an especially rich grouping. As an example the Chaconne for Violin will serve:

and the D-minor Suite for Cello:

In the introduction to the duet "Verzage nicht, O Häuflein klein" from Cantata 42, the articulation of the bass part with its dots (trembling), both accented and unaccented slurrings of notes (entreaties and sighs), give eloquent expression to these ideas even before the entrance of the voices:

110

Especially famous is the change of articulation noted by Spitta in the duet *Et in unum Dominum Jesum Christum* from the B-minor Mass, where the same motif, differently articulated, expresses the idea that the Father and Son are of the same substance but appear in different forms:

111
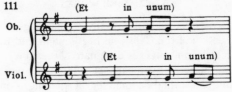

In the alto aria from Cantata 79 (*Gott der Herr ist Sonn und Schild*) the obbligato part (oboe or flute) is unmarked; when it is used in the A-major Mass (violins and violas in unison), it is richly decorated through articulation. A similar instance is the carefully marked obbligato violin part to the embellished chorale "Lobe den Herren, der alles so mächtig regieret" from Cantata 137, which Bach later took over, without markings, into the six so-called Schübler Chorales for organ. Here the player may write the missing articulation into his copy from the cantata. The pianist, too, should study and transfer intelligently to his own instrument the almost inexhaustible richness of these groupings, as shown in our examples; he will be astonished to discover that Bach's melodic line will take on a living quality of which he previously had no idea!

⋙ ⋙ ⋙ ⋘ ⋘ ⋘

Articulation in the Unmarked
Clavier and Organ Music of Bach

A. CLAVIER WORKS

In Bach's early works we find virtually no markings whatever, except in the lament section of the Capriccio in B♭ major and in the F♯ minor Toccata, in which a movement is designated "Presto e staccato." In the Inventions (1723), too — by means of which the performer "should above all acquire a cantabile manner of playing" — melodic, legato playing is indicated by slurs only in the Two-Part Inventions in D major and F minor; furthermore, in several of the Three-Part Inventions a firm legato linkage of notes is not always technically possible (for example at the end of the G-major Invention). The first volume of the *Well-Tempered Clavier* remained entirely unmarked (up to the subject of the B-minor Fugue) — a welcome playground for countless editors! Also, the suites, apart from a pair of small slurs, show almost no markings (the beginning of the fourth English Suite is marked in the *Urtext* edition by Kreutz with staccato dots, which were removed in two later editions and can scarcely be regarded as original). The few markings in the *Italian Concerto* are obviously violinistic in the first movement:

112

etc. and

and so forth (for strings Bach would probably have written

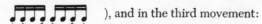), and in the third movement:

The second movement of this work is also to be performed like the solo of a violin concerto accompanied by a string quartet.

In the first of the Duets (1739) the continuous beam takes the place of the missing legato slur:

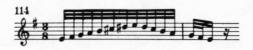

In the second book of the *Well-Tempered Clavier* (1744) there are characteristic wedges in the subjects of the figures in E minor, F major, and A minor. In the three-voiced Ricercare from the *Musical Offering* (1747) our attention is called to the lightly dancing quarter notes in the countersubject to the theme:

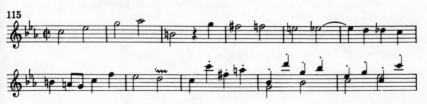

This short review shows that Bach attached more significance to articulation in his later works, but also that from a stylistic point of view, these few points of reference are insufficient for an interpretation of the majority of the remaining unmarked works. Furthermore, conclusion by analogy from the cantatas and chamber works is not admissible in every case, above all not in the youthful works, which still were strongly influenced by Middle and North German clavier and organ music. Also, it is clear that the harpsichord demands a different style of articulation than does the clavichord, and the modern piano — on which Bach is most often played — requires yet another. Thus general rules that have validity for all three instruments cannot be stated dogmatically; instead we can only suggest general principles, which can be deduced from the music itself. Such suggested articulations, which are presented to the reader and player as no more than points of reference to help him come to his own conclusions, may now be given for the fugue subjects from the *Well-Tempered Clavier*. Musical examples may be omitted because everyone should own the music and have it at hand.

The Well-Tempered Clavier
BOOK ONE

No. 1, C major: As already stated above (page 25), this model fugue is best performed with the normal articulation in such a way that the seconds are slurred, the fourths and fifths set apart from one another, portato.

No. 2, C minor: The continuous *pp e sempre staccato* of Czerny (suitable for Beethoven, but not Bach) is generally disregarded today. The sixteenths are slurred, the eighths, according to the interpretation of the fugue, either lightly or expressively detached.

No. 3, C♯ major: The fugue can be interpreted either quietly (delicately) or with motion (elegantly): the degree of the staccato of the eighth depends upon this.

No. 4, C♯ minor: The first subject in heavy legato, portamento; the second (eighth-note) subject in a relaxed legato; the third (upbeat) with a slurring of the fourth.

No. 5, D major: The dotted eighths separated as in a French overture; the sixteenths in measure 9:

No. 6, D minor: The rise of the eighth notes and the soaring of the sixteenths lead to the climax, B♭, which, in Gerber's copy, is marked with a wedge.

No. 7, E♭ major: For the eighth notes in the first measure, one must think in terms of wedges; for those in the second measure, dots; articulate the remainder as in the *Italian Concerto:*

No. 8, E♭ minor: No caesura in the second measure! Either all the notes strongly slurred, or the fifths and fourths in a softly portamentoed legato.

No. 9, E major: Upbeat staccato (see page 39).

No. 10, E minor: Non-legato; in the second measure slurred groups of three: E–D♯–E and G–F♯–G.

No. 11, F major: If the upbeat is slurred, the following eighth notes should have a gentle portato.

No. 12, F minor: Legato; the tension of the melody should not be dissipated in the motif in seconds (see Example 89).

No. 13, F♯ major: The beginning as in No. 11; the end:

No. 14, F♯ minor: The little caesuras after the first and fourth quarters of the second measure almost imperceptible; otherwise everything legato.

No. 15, G major: The eighth notes detached in fiery fashion, the sixteenths loosely slurred; the excessive slurring of the quarter notes C to B and E to D found in many editions originated with Czerny.

No. 16, G minor: In the first measure, D – E♭ and F♯ – G slurred; in the second measure B♭ – G markedly detached.

No. 17, A♭ major: In a heavy portamentoed legato.

No. 18, G♯ minor: Legato up until the repeated notes:

No. 19, A major: One can either slur this remarkable theme throughout, or articulate with stress on the strong beats thus:

No. 20, A minor: The eighth notes portato; however, at G♯ – E, wedges (as in No. 7) and the last four eighths as in No. 13.

No. 21, B♭ major: The seconds D – C, and E♭ – D legato; the sixths separated; the eighth notes of the first measure, which in the second are divided into sixteenths, should also be detached; caesuras after the first eighth of the second and third measures.

No. 22, B♭ minor: The half notes heavily portamentoed, the quarter notes legato.

No. 23, B major: Legato except for the second quarter in the second measure   ♩♩   Caesura in the first measure after the C♯.

No. 24, B minor: The slurs over the suspended eighth notes in the first and second measures are in the autograph; the broken chords F♯ – D – B and (third measure) C♯ – A – F♯ in a heavy portato.

The Well-Tempered Clavier
BOOK TWO

No. 1, C major: The eighth notes sharply detached, the sixteenths lightly, the quarter notes accented.

No. 2 C minor: Expressively slurred.

No. 3, C♯ major: The eighth notes detached, with accent.

No. 4, C♯ minor: In a loose legato, the chromatic second theme legato.

No. 5, D major: No caesura at the beginning of the second measure; the quarter notes G – B and F♯ – D detached, with accent.

No. 6, D minor: A sharp caesura before the chromatically falling line; the end as in Nos. 13 and 20 of Book I.

No. 7, E♭ major: Apart from the fifth, which is detached and accented at the beginning, everything else is legato.

No. 8, D♯ minor: Gently legato throughout.

No. 9, E major: In a strict legato.

No. 10, E minor: The original wedges over the unslurred quarters of the first four measures are enough of a guide.

No. 11, F major: Here also there are original wedges over the eighth notes.

No. 12, F minor: Slur the upbeat, detach the other eighths more lightly or more heavily according to interpretation.

No. 13, F♯ major: The quarter note in the first measure sharply detached, in the third measure detached in a springy manner.

No. 14, F♯ minor: The upbeats $c\sharp^2$, a^1, $f\sharp^1$ in the third measure detached; the remainder legato.

No. 15, G major: Leggiero scherzando.

No. 16, G minor: The quarters and the eighths detached heavily and with pathos.

No. 17, A♭ major: Very legato, no caesura at the octave leap.

No. 18, G♯ minor: One should imagine a not-too-thick legato slur over the first three eighth notes of the first and third measures.

No. 19, A major: Legato, except for 𝅘𝅥𝅮𝅘𝅥𝅮𝅘𝅥𝅮 𝅘𝅥𝅮𝅘𝅥𝅮𝅘𝅥𝅮 in the first measure.

No. 20, A minor: The wedges over the eighth notes of the subject are in the autograph. The quarter notes too require a weighty, accented detachment.

No. 21, B♭ major: The little slurs over the second and third quarters of the third and fourth measures are in the autograph. Accordingly the first quarter should be detached; also after the first eighth of the second measure a separation may, but need not, be made.

No. 22, B♭ minor: The half notes in the first measure, the quarter notes $d\flat^1$ in the first, c^1 in the second, f^1 and g^1 in the fourth measure are to be separated.

No. 23, B major: Connect firmly the subject and its continuation.

No. 24, B minor: Like No. 11 in Book I.

B. ORGAN WORKS

Articulation on the organ is even more important than on the clavier, for two reasons: first, because the legato style is used more in playing the organ than in playing any other instrument, and second, because on the organ accent can be created only through articulation.

It has already been mentioned (page 33) that in the course of the seventeenth century legato playing came more and more to be required; this requirement was first fulfilled in Bach's time through the perfection of keyboard technique (passing the thumb under, equal employment of all the fingers). A faultless legato is rightly regarded as the soul of organ playing; and yet, the organ cannot ignore articulation. Some themes of Bach, such as the beginning of the C-major Toccata

would immediately become unintelligible if played legato, when it would sound like

Only if the two first notes are slightly detached does one hear the last one as accented. If, in the subject of the "Great" G-minor Fugue, the upbeat eighth note is detached, the strong beats of the measure receive a natural accent; if it is slurred over, there arises a kind of counter-accent:

This effect will be particularly noted in descending scale passages, whereas in rising melodies, as at the beginning of the C-minor Fantasy (III, 6) even when the upbeat is slurred the main note retains the accent. Since the sound of the organ does not die away like that of the clavier, a very slight interruption is sufficient to be perceptible. Consequently, in the music of Bach it is not good either to slur everything that can be slurred, or in repetitions of a note, to shorten the note to half its value, as the older French School (Dupré) does. The organist must have at his disposal more greatly differentiated degrees of separation of notes than the pianist; a "skipping" staccato, which some organ virtuosos prefer, is neither suitable to the dignity of the instrument, nor does it sound effective, for the pipes have too little time to speak. Articulation rather than the agogic prolongations Riemann prescribed must take over the meaningful accent on the organ.

If, in the "Great" G-minor Fugue, the subject is thoughtfully phrased (see page 71) and carefully articulated, if the first obbligato counter-subject is performed legatissimo, the second in an open non-legato, everything in this famous and much-played fugue will sound rhythmic-ally clear of its own accord, and one will not need either to agitate it excessively or to dress it up through registration.

In the organ works, too, it is in his later style that Bach gives us rather more points of reference for articulation. There are, in the youth-ful works, several instances where he paid tribute to the style of *reper-cussio* that sprang up about 1700. Here the violinistic effect of repeated notes is taken over on the organ, not always happily (Lübeck, Fugue in D minor; Buxtehude, Fugue in A minor; and others). In Bach this occurs in the Fugues in E major (III, 7), G minor (III, 5) and the Violin transcription in D minor (III, 4). In all of these cases, the eighth notes must be uniformly, but only slightly, detached. This is valid also for the Passacaglia, which in the counterpoint

(as Bach himself directs) must only be slurred from E♭ to B and not from B to C too.

A strong differentiation between organ and clavier style can be first distinguished in Bach's music in the *Orgelbüchlein* (1717) and in the *Well-Tempered Clavier* (1722). However, we still find thereafter or-ganistic subjects among the clavier works (Prelude in E♭ major, Fugue in B minor in the first book of the *Well-Tempered Clavier*), and clavier-istic themes in the organ works (the middle section of the Passacaglia). Original marking is found in several of the movements of the six Trio Sonatas for two manuals and pedal, and only occasionally in the Third Part of the *Klavierübung*: in the Prelude in E♭ major (see Example 101), in the fughetta on *Allein Gott in der Höh sei Ehr*, where the dots over the eighth notes symbolize the ascending and descending angels, and in the great and profound version of *Vater unser in Himmelreich* (VII, 52), where the "Lombard sighs" are said to express anxiety, and the staccato triplets to express the weakness and helplessness of man-kind lost in this world. In the six Schübler Chorales (1746), of which five are transcriptions from cantatas, Bach repeated the original articulation indications in only one case (*Wachet auf, ruft uns die Stimme,* see Example 97); for the articulation of the others, the player can consult the original versions (in the cantatas, see page 83).

If the original organ works remained almost unmarked, the organ parts to the cantatas (Nos. 27, 29, 35, 47, 49, 71, 146, 169, 170, 172, and 188) are in many cases marked very carefully. The organ, which in these examples for the most part substitutes for a missing melodic instrument, has only a single-voiced ornamented melody line to perform, and articulates it as would a melodic instrument, as the following measures from Cantata 47 show:

120

Naturally, one ought not to transfer a marking of this sort automatically to the original organ works, but it does show how differentiated an articulation Bach required from the organ too, when there was need. Anyone who wonders whether and how the gigantic curves of the two manual parts at the beginning of the Toccata in F major should be articulated, can perhaps take as a model the introduction to an aria from Cantata 39, which is in the same key and meter:

121

Without excluding other possibilities, the beginning of the Toccata in F major could then be marked in the following fashion (provided that only a very small differentiation be made between legato and non-legato):

Further examples can be omitted, for intelligent organists can perceive everything fundamental in the examples given so far — and will indeed reserve the decision in each individual case to themselves.

CHAPTER TEN

❯❯❯ ❯❯❯ ❯❯❯ ❮❮❮ ❮❮❮ ❮❮❮

Articulation in the Works
of Mozart

THE RADICAL change in style between the Baroque and Classical periods, which was heralded about 1730 and can be considered completed by about 1770, transformed to a greater or lesser degree almost all the expressive elements of music. Certain typical forms of expression withdraw into the background, such as the broken rhythm of the French overture, Handel's *Largo e staccato,* the articulation of groups in Bach's great melodic line, the slurring of two notes on a strong beat; to offset this loss, articulation, together with dynamics, tempo, and tone color, was increasingly raised to the status of an independent area of expression, a development that reached its temporary zenith and conclusion with Beethoven. It is not possible within the limits of the present work to undertake a special consideration of the style of articulation of the Mannheim School or of that of Gluck and Haydn; we must limit ourselves to two high points, Mozart and Beethoven. If Mozart has remained unsurpassed in the refinement and unpredictability of his phrasing and articulation, Beethoven, like no one before or after him, forced from them effects of an elemental nature.

In Mozart we see an almost complete unity of art and life. His personality comes through to us just as clearly from the course of his life and from his letters as from his music. His directness, the total lack of calculation (in art: of reflection), the tendency to yield to every idea, every feeling that so perniciously influenced his life, all these traits are reflected in his music, too, where we are frequently surprised by the changes of mood, the irregularity of his phrase structure, the apparent caprice of articulation (see Examples 8, 9, 10, 67-72). Not only in the string quartets and symphonies but in the piano works as well, there is a richness of articulation that inspired Wiehmayer to write: "The sonatas of Mozart contain a surprising abundance of the finest articulation, which, appropriately performed, lends to the playing something of the brilliance and sparkle of true polished crystal. Erase the written articulations from these compositions and you erase that heavenly grace and lightness which charms us so much in the works of this master; the performance takes on the dull and flat effect of a glass imitation." Certainly only the performer who possesses an *Urtext* edition has this pleasure, for with Mozart more than any other Classical composer, editors until very recently have held it to be their right to substitute their own markings for the original ones (see Examples 149 through 152). Moreover, in the early editions the staccato signs in particular are unreliable, owing to reasons having to do with the convenience of the engraver; further, there are many works that Mozart reserved for his own personal use (such as the piano concertos of the Viennese period) which he left largely unmarked so that one must rely for guidance upon those works that he himself marked precisely and which are available in autograph manuscripts (such as the Rondo in A minor for piano).

The filigree style of the Viennese Classical period does not permit an articulation of groups within the grand melodic line as in Bach. Instead, contrasts between legato and staccato are more prominent. Occasionally Mozart uses them in pure mischievousness, as in the Sonata in C major (K. 279):

Sometimes the dynamic marking piano occurs together with legato, and forte together with staccato, as in the second theme of the finale of the *Jupiter Symphony* or in the Sonata in F major (K. 280):

Frequently, as in the Sonata in A major (K. 331), staccato scales fly upwards to conclude surprisingly in legato:

Mozart does not always differentiate between wedge and dot, but when he does it is often in a very characteristic manner, as in the Overture to *Don Giovanni*, where Don Juan and Zerlina contend with one another:

Often there are wedges in the forte passages and dots in piano passages, as in the Sonata in G major (K. 283):

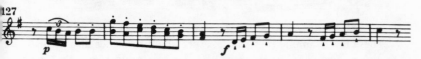

In the theme of the four-hands Variations in G major (K. 501) the wedge is over a long note to indicate an accent (the Peters edition substitutes *tenuto* for it):

A high-spirited, unpredictable change from two slurred to two separated notes is exhibited in the finale of the Symphony in E♭ major (K. 543):

In the String Quartet in F major (K. 590) the articulation of the repeated notes C, B♭, A is presented in breathtaking contrast:

Similarly in the little Gigue (K. 547), where the articulation temporarily
threatens to suspend the ⁶⁄₈ rhythm:

As one would expect, the ornamented melodies of the Adagio movements often contain the most exquisite articulation (Sonata in F major,
K. 280):

These few examples may suffice, especially if reference also be made
to those given earlier. However, Beethoven's critical remark, which
Czerny reports to us, ought to be mentioned: Mozart has "a fine but
'cut up' manner of playing, no *ligato*." Beethoven could have heard
Mozart only once, during his short first visit to Vienna in the winter of
1786-87. That Mozart should have had no legato must be reckoned as
out of the question; it is possible, however, that to the aging Beethoven's recollection, Mozart's style of playing seemed all too precious,
and that indeed the significantly improved piano of Beethoven's day
permitted a more songlike legato. At the same time, however, in this
criticism is expressed the profound internal difference between the two
masters.

CHAPTER ELEVEN

❯❯❯ ❯❯❯ ❯❯❯ ❰❰❰ ❰❰❰ ❰❰❰

Articulation in the Works
of Beethoven

IN SPITE of their proximity in time and style, two more contrasting masters than Mozart and Beethoven can hardly be imagined. Beethoven's style is masculine by contrast to the feminine style of Mozart. Just as Mozart shows a spiritual relationship with Goethe, so Beethoven's art is infused with an idealism reminiscent of Schiller. His themes are terser, more pregnant with meaning than Mozart's; their development is animated by a tension of will that is foreign to Mozart; his harmony favors the simplest degrees of the tonality; his dynamics employ strong contrasts; his phrasing prefers the parenthetical, the precipitous fall (see Examples 11, 14, 15, 17, 19, 23-25); his style of articulation does not know the refinement of Mozart's, but has a profound grasp of the character and contrast of legato and staccato and uses them with elemental effectiveness.

As early as in the three youthful sonatas dedicated to the Elector of Cologne (1781), the carefully stereotyped articulation (for the most part ♪♪♪♪) is striking. The depth of contrast between legato and staccato is illustrated especially in the slow movements of the first piano sonatas, such as Opus 7, where in the quiet-after-anxiety of the *pp* sustained diminished seventh chord, the *ff* blows strike like flashing lightning — and after the terrifying rest how fervently the melody enters again, legato!

133 Largo con gran espressione

In the Largo of the Sonata, Opus 2, No. 2 (and frequently elsewhere) the soprano *(tenuto sempre)* is opposed to the stabbing steps of the bass *(staccato sempre)*. Although one might cite further examples from the sonatas (see Examples 30, 32, 33, and 36), Beethoven's style of articulation reached its highest development in the symphonies and in the program overtures. Above all, it is the scherzo movements of the symphonies that can be regarded as the apotheosis of the staccato; their character is unbound in the highest sense, and conveys to the hearer that intoxicating sensation of strength and freedom that only Beethoven was able to give us. In the Fourth Symphony (which has found no such champion as the Seventh had in Richard Wagner) the contrast between the introduction and the first movement is that between connection and separation (as in Goethe's *Meeresstille und glückliche Fahrt*): the dense veil of the introduction is raised by the short gusts of the rising wind, and in the Allegro vivace the ship flies before the wind. In the second theme there is an interesting linking of phrases through articulation:

134

In the repetition, forte, the articulation is energetically altered while the phrase linkage remains in effect:

135

True marvels in articulation are to be found in the development of the first movement, where, through 24 measures of a continuous harmony E – G – B♭, together with the diminuendo from *ff* to *pp* there is a change from staccato to legato and an enharmonic change to B major. In the second movement, there is the contrast of the legato melody and the detached dotted rhythm; in the third, the conflict of the slurring of twos with the rhythm of three; in the finale, it is the fast, detached sixteenths (which in one place are even entrusted to the bassoon), that round out the picture of this "articulation symphony." For Beethoven's use of the staccato for dramatic purposes, two famous examples may be given. The first is from the end of the Funeral March of the *Eroica,* where the chief subject halts, staggers as if broken, and finally sinks down:

The second example is taken from the Fifth Symphony, where the theme of the third movement reappears in the finale, *pp* and pizzicato, as ghostly as the spirit of Banquo at the feast — one of the places where Beethoven and Shakespeare draw close to one another:

The second movement twice shows a striking change of articulation, perhaps related to a program of this movement unknown to us (Grove).

Of the overtures, let us examine that to the tragedy *Coriolanus* by Collin. This overture is an inspired encapsulation of the drama. It shows us the embittered old Roman who was restrained by his mother from going over to the enemy. The unison of the beginning is like a long repressed outbreak of anger,

the eighth notes, rising staccato, then falling legato, show his vacillation,

the second, songlike theme depicts the pleas of the mother; the end is exhaustion and resignation — need one, after this music, see the drama itself?

What was said concerning the notation of slurs in Mozart is also generally true of Beethoven: the editors have not concerned themselves greatly about the original markings, but have changed Beethoven's markings in countless instances at their own discretion, as the current popular editions of the time before the First World War show. Scarcely an editor had the courage to let Beethoven's slurs stand, as in the theme for the Variations in the Sonata, Opus 109:

The two-measure phrases are understandable by themselves, but the slurring of measures four and five, which bridges over the end of the phrase, is not obvious. It demonstrates an inner compulsion motivated by the crescendo in the fourth measure — at the end of the sonata, where the theme enters once more quietly, transfigured, both the crescendo and the slur are missing.

In his early works Beethoven does not distinguish significantly between wedge and dot. There are sonatas with dots throughout, others with wedges. Thus the Sonata, Opus 10, No. 2 is marked entirely throughout with wedges, which in the lightly moving finale give a bristling appearance:

Here, and in numerous other passages where only one kind of sign is used, dots might better have corresponded to the character of the music. In his valuable study "Punkte oder Striche?" ("Dots or Strokes?"), Nottebohm (*Beethoveniana*, I, p. 107 ff.) expresses the opinion that

Beethoven, in distinguishing the two signs, was not thinking of the various methods of violin bowing or the various articulations of the woodwinds, but that he was in agreement with what the piano methods of the beginning of the nineteenth century (Clementi, Starke) wanted to express with the stroke (wedge), "that a note marked with a stroke [wedge] should be played sharper or shorter than one marked with a dot." This can however only refer to the piano music, for in his orchestral music Beethoven used the wedge in the old sense — that is, to indicate a normal staccato, as when he instructs the copyist, in the Allegretto of the Seventh Symphony, to write not

142

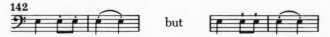

but

Furthermore, Nottebohm mentions a letter written by Beethoven in 1825 to Karl Holz on the occasion of the publication of the Quartet in A minor, Opus 132: "Where • [a dot] stands over the note, there should be no ▼ [wedge] in its place — 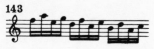 is not the same as ." One cannot express himself more clearly, and yet Karl Krebs, in the foreword to his *Urtext* edition of Beethoven's Piano Sonatas, stated that in the autograph of the quartet there are only wedges, that Beethoven consequently became aware of the difference only during publication of the quartet!

Still another interesting excerpt from a letter may be quoted, showing how Beethoven in his care for the education of his nephew Karl, also concerned himself with the problem of articulation in piano playing. He wrote to Czerny, Karl's piano teacher: "In certain passages such as

143

I should like him also to use all his fingers now and then, and in such passages too as

so that he may connect [the notes]. Admittedly such passages sound, as they say, as if they were 'played like pearls (i.e. with less finger action) or like a single pearl' [now, with a true Beethovenian turn] occasionally we like to have a different kind of jewelry"! From this quotation one sees that by about 1820 the modern concept of virtuoso piano style was to sacrifice the legato to the more brilliant non-legato technique.

≫≫ ≫≫ ≫≫ ≪≪ ≪≪ ≪≪

The Nineteenth Century

AFTER THE extraordinary growth that tempo, dynamics, phrasing, and articulation experienced as independent areas of expression in music toward the end of the eighteenth century, the nineteenth century at first shows not only no further growth but a movement backward instead. This century — much and often unjustly abused — can be judged from different points of view. Here the development of music in the period after the Viennese Classical composers will be approached from the point of view of its widespread popularization, in which the piano has the chief role. There is almost always a loss in depth connected with an extension in breadth; the middle-class dilettante of 1830 possessed neither the education nor the taste of the *nobile dilettante* of the eighteenth century, and the patronage of the new ruling class of high finance was painfully different from that of the aristocracy that had sponsored Haydn and Beethoven. While virtuosity — on the piano because of Liszt and on the violin because of Paganini — was raised to incredible heights, in substance the bravura variations and the opera fantasies of the time remain far below the standards the eighteenth century had set for light, recreational music. So, too, in the areas of phrasing and articulation instead of progress, there was a regression. The formal construction of most of the single-movement piano pieces of the Romantic period is, in the large sense as well as in detail more primitive than in Mozart; large forms in the Romantic period originate chiefly through the addition of smaller forms to one another (especially with Schumann), and these movements, for the most part, are constructed of four-measure phrases, without the frequent changes and irregularities of Mozart. To be sure, the harmony becomes

richer, but the formal design becomes weaker. It is not until the second
half of the century that music again achieves — especially through
those two opposites, Brahms and Wagner — a longer breath. Brahms
reaches over the Viennese Classical composers back to Bach and the
older polyphony. Wagner has, in his orchestral language, increased to
the ultimate the reach of his "endless melody" by ceaseless phrase-link-
ages from one instrument to another. Bruckner did not follow his master
Wagner in this respect, but, for the most part, lets one theme die away
completely before a new one arises; Reger, on the other hand, with
his motifs organized from small elements is, in phrasing, to be considered a disciple of Brahms.

As regards the notation of phrasing, composers in the nineteenth
century too scorned the use of the special signs that were offered them
by the theorists of the eighteenth century; only rarely do they use
diagonal double strokes (which had been used once by Beethoven in
his posthumously published Piano Trio in E♭ major) in order to
emphasize an especially declamatory section.

Articulation too did not develop beyond Mozart and Beethoven; it
goes without saying, of course, that there was no attempt to take up
again Bach's bold articulation of groups. This state of affairs may be
observed especially in the studies by Czerny and Cramer, who, however
many technical problems they raise and work out in exercises, handle
articulation only incidentally and conventionally. With the great composers, it is hardly different. We find in Schubert an unquenchable
source of exquisite melodies, true marvels in harmony; but the modest
tension that had such a negative effect for Schubert's middle-class
existence shows itself also in a modest formal grasp and a often dull
articulation. The articulation of Weber's piano music is to be understood as derived partly from the opera, partly from the brilliant style
of high-flown salon music. Mendelssohn, with the fairy music from
A Midsummer Night's Dream and in several instrumental pieces influenced by that work, raised the exquisite light staccato to an expressive
height the Classical composers had not known. In Schumann, in the
genius period of his first piano works, we find some articulations full of
fantasy in the pieces designated *Paganini* and *Reconnaissance* from the
Carnaval; in the imitation of the bouncing bow of the violin in the
third of the *Symphonic Études.*

In punctuated rhythms he favored the pattern ♩ 𝄾 ♩♩ 𝄾 ♩♪

(Intermezzi, Opus 3, No. 1; *Davidsbündlertänze*, Opus 6, No. 9; Sonata
in F♯ minor, Opus 11, third and fourth movements; see also Example
29).

With the classic composer of Romantic piano music, Chopin, the regular use of four-measure phrases is immediately striking; phrase overlappings are rare; however, phrase linkages are to be found, especially in the Mazurkas (see Example 11). Like most of composers of his time, Chopin prefers to draw legato slurs from the beginning to the end of a phrase, and consequently conceives these slurs at the same time as phrasing marks. He makes the heavy chords at the end of the Ballade in F minor visually obvious through the separation of the individual eighth notes:

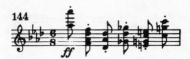

He uses the wedge, again especially in the Mazurkas, for a vigorous staccato, particularly in downward leaps. Liszt's al-fresco style also shows itself in the articulation; he uses the wedge especially to articulate hammered-out octaves (Sonata in B minor).

We encounter a classically schooled, nuanced construction of phrase and style of articulation again only in Brahms (see Examples 16, 21, 26, and 63). Especially in his orchestral works, Brahms usually limits the slurs as the Classical composers had done. In addition to the example from the Second Symphony given in Chapter Five, we cite the beginning of the Violin Concerto, Opus 77:

In the finale of the First Symphony, the slur in the violins ends at the barline, while in the cellos and basses it is carried over:

This example shows also an especially beautiful transfer from legato to staccato together with dynamic intensification: the slurs become shorter, cease entirely, and in their place enters the accented syncopation which disappears in the staccato. Brahms used the reverse pattern in the first movement of the same symphony; the wedges become dots together with the diminuendo, the non-legato carries over into the slurs:

All these beautiful effects lie open to view, and yet it is perhaps not superfluous to call attention to them. Brahms uses the wedge in his orchestral works not only to indicate a shortening, but also to indicate forcible accent, while on the other hand, in the third movement of his Sonata, Opus 1 he prefers to indicate the *staccatissimo* by dots.

We cannot here go into the wealth of articulation that is to be found in the works of Richard Wagner. One can view Wagner's development as the constant refining of a style that was, in the beginning, fairly crude: there is a vast distance from the first attempts to *Tristan* and *Die Meistersinger*. As Wagner — who cherished nothing more than theatrical effects — learned to master the total operatic language of his time and raise himself above it, so is his articulation less original than exceedingly exacting with respect to all the instruments. It is not the manner in which he articulates, but what he is able to express with it that makes Wagner the towering master he is once more recognized to be today, after a period of reaction against him.

Bruckner, in his symphonies, articulates after the model of Wagner; he marks the parts of his symphonies with a confidence that has something touching in it, as when, in the Ninth Symphony, he uses a combination of slur, dot, and portato strokes:

148

Tchaikovsky dared to write a whole movement for strings pizzicato *(Pizzicato ostinato)* in the scherzo of the Fourth Symphony, in F minor. Reger liked to draw over his works a thick net of slurs — sometimes legato marks, sometimes phrasing marks — which strengthen still further the thoughtful character of his music. But he also cultivated the staccato side as few others did, especially in the scherzo movements of his chamber music, and in the closing fugues usually beginning *pp e sempre staccato,* of his great variation works. He was especially fond of the form ♩♩♩♩ . After the first performance of the *Overture to a Comedy,* one of his weaker works, a musician was asked on the next day: "Well, how did it go?" "Oh — two legato, two staccato notes," was the answer.

Within the framework of the present work we cannot go into the further development of articulation at the beginning of the twentieth century, particularly as it is found in the Impressionistic piano music of Debussy and Ravel, or developed further, in the string quartets of Béla Bartók. For practical performance — that is, for those practices that might be changed and improved through suggestion and criticism, the point in the development in the nineteenth century lies not in what its composers created but rather with the editors of Classical music for instructional purposes — editions that were also used almost exclusively in the home and in the concert hall. The constantly increasing numbers and interest of musical amateurs demanded every sort of marked edition, complete with fingerings and performance indications of every kind, and the business of furnishing these trimmings kept growing up to the end of the century. In literature, the school editions of the classics with commentaries were used only in the schools, and misused as materials of learning, but in the bookcases at home were the unannotated original editions, to which one could turn if he were seeking enjoyment rather than instruction. In music, however, the edited and revised editions of music had so supplanted the original in the course of the nineteenth century that I remember about 1900 I could never

secure a single other edition of Bach, Handel, Haydn, Mozart, Beethoven, even of Schubert and other works available for reprinting
in the nineteenth century to look at or play from than these edited
popular editions of the major music publishers. Czerny may be regarded
as founder of this movement; in 1837 he began to bring out the clavier
works of Bach in an edition complete with fingerings, tempo, dynamic,
and articulation marks, as well as with other added indications for
performance; and he quickly found numerous imitators and disciples.
It is easy to sit in judgment on these editions today, and to condemn
the stylelessness in their editing; for all that, they had meaning for
their times and for the average amateur and piano teacher of those
days, whose attainments were very modest by our standards. What
Czerny did for the pianists, Ferdinand David did in his *Hohe Schule
des Violinspiels* for the violinists. The editors of these instructive editions were, for the most part, well-intentioned, even important musicians, who, on commission from a publisher, and with the needs of the
public in mind, sought to complete and improve the original text
"according to the most up-to-date requirements." In none of these cases
was a distinction made between the markings of the composer and
those of the editor, so that no one could know whether a tempo indication, a forte or a piano, a slur, a dot (wedges were no longer used) a
crescendo or a diminuendo stemmed from the composer or from the
editor. Thus, to give only two examples, the theme of Mozart's Sonata
in A major, which reads as follows in the original:

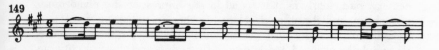

was "phrased" in the Peters edition (No. 9268) in the following fashion:

not only suppressing Mozart's few original marks, but changing the
light grace of the theme into something emotional, not to say senti-
mental. (Reger, in his Variations on this theme also uses it in this
corrupt form at the beginning, but in the repetition marks it differently.)

The second example concerns the theme of the *Eroica Variations*,
Opus 35, of Beethoven, which the composer slurred violinistically in
the piano version as he did in the symphony:

In the edition mentioned the slurs are changed as follows:

What holes in the second and fourth measures!

After 1900, the phrasing slurs began to overgrow musical notation in unwholesome fashion. In his very important and thoughtful edition of the second volume of Bach's organ works (Peters), Karl Straube occasionally draws two, even three, slurs of different lengths, over one another, underneath which often a pair of staccato dots struggle for some air; similarly, Otto Barblan, in his new edition of the organ works of César Franck (also published by Peters) covered the composer's clear notation by a system of totally superfluous phrasing slurs. One might perhaps ask: Why are these slurs superfluous? Do they not give the player, from the outset, a clear picture of the intended cohesion of the phrase construction, of the combination of phrases and motifs into larger structures? That cannot be denied; but they smother the articulation; and every player who studies a work will quickly find the intended correlations. Once one has the music correctly conceived in his mind, he can read its expression from the notation. The worst damage done by these editions, however, was to the older, unmarked music, which often permits more than one interpretation. Here, the performer using a marked edition has no alternative but to take the editor's interpretation as his own.

That dangers and misunderstandings were present here was seen clearly in the nineteenth century by certain courageous people, who undertook to swim against the stream. As early as 1862 Franz Kroll made the music world a present of an *Urtext* edition of the *Well-Tempered Clavier* (on which the Peters edition based its popular editions, *Volksausgabe* No. 1, a and b), but how few were then competent to play from it! After 1880, there appeared, as a carefully edited and stylistically well-grounded edition of the keyboard works of Bach, the version of F. Bischoff in the Steingräber edition, which added to the original text (after Bischoff's own study of sources) only a few performance indications in small type. After 1900, the *Urtext* editions of

Classical works appeared, published by the Prussian Academy of Arts in Berlin. It was an undertaking of great value but it received only a weak response. Only after World War I, as the singing and playing groups of the youth movement accelerated a renaissance of old music — in which we still find ourselves — these young people categorically demanded that older music no longer be experienced through the medium of the middle-class nineteenth century, but rather directly in its own right, and in its own appropriate style. They wanted to perform the older music from an original text, or, where that was not convenient (for example, because the figured bass must be filled in) from an edition in which the original text and the sometimes necessary additions of the editor were clearly differentiated from one another. Those who prepared the way and who were the leaders in this battle were the publishers well grounded in this kind of editing, especially Bärenreiter — who published the original German version of the present work, which might be viewed as a continuation of this struggle — and Kallmeyer. Other publishers soon associated themselves with the movement: *Nagels Musikarchiv,* the collection *Organum* which Seiffert published, the collection *Antiqua* in Schott's catalogue, the *Urtext* editions of Bach's works by Peters, recently those of G. Henle, and a host of others. For a time the pendulum, as it almost always does in such movements, swung too strongly in the other direction: performers wanted to play the older music as objectively as possible, to nip in the bud every suspicion of a "romantic" performance; they thought they could renounce nuance altogether, because no markings were present, and especially with respect to tempo, dynamics, and articulation therefore played as expressionlessly as possible. People soon learned, however, especially through the writings of Schering and Haas about performance practice in older music, that in such music too, great demands were made on performers, only of a different sort from those of the nineteenth century. Thus we seek today to reconquer the traditions in which this music lived. A good deal has been won, a good deal achieved; more remains to be done. It is necessary to revive the colorful timbres of the old settings, to remove from figured bass the school dust of theoretical instruction, to make the old improvisatory ornamental style alive again. One problem is to recognize the significance of phrasing and articulation for the performance of older music, to distinguish both areas clearly, and to set up basic principles according to which unmarked music of the seventeenth and eighteenth centuries can be intelligently articulated. How much of this must still be done has been shown by the present work, which may have raised more questions than it has given definite answers. Everyone hears whether a performer plays wrong notes in a well-known Classical work — but does one also hear whether he phrases incorrectly or articulates capriciously? The premises on which to base a performance that is at once stylistically irreproachable and artistically on a high level must be created here. It is very gratifying that *Urtext* editions appear today in increasing number, and are demanded; but, creditable and necessary as they are, only a small number of musical amateurs and professionals so far is capable of breathing life into the dead notational symbols of an *Urtext* edition of older music. The editions of the nineteenth century have been done away with; between these and the pure *Urtext* editions — at least for the seventeenth century and the time of Bach — we need an in-between solution: editions marked sparsely and true to style, which permit the original text to be clearly distinguished, yet spare the performer gross misconceptions without taking from him in the least the joy of discovery. As a model edition of the sort might be cited the edition of Mozart's Violin Sonatas by Schnabel and Flesch (Peters), in which the editors have grasped and expressed the spirit of Mozart wonderfully in their additions, printed in small type.

Nor should I neglect the interpretative editions of highly gifted musicians, such as those of Bülow, Busoni, and Straube (to name only three), which one might call "hyphenated editions": Bach-Busoni, Beethoven-Bülow, Bach-Straube; one experiences the great composer through the mediation of a great interpreter, whom one need not follow but who nevertheless shows the player things he might not have seen for himself. Finally, let it be said that in every performance two factors must be distinguished: one objective, with which knowledge, education, and practice are concerned; and one subjective which arises from the fact that for each person the world, even the spiritual world, looks a little different than it does to the others. It happens that we can only transfer ourselves with certainty back into that world of music which is not more than two or three hundred years past. For being able to do it at all, we are indebted to the capacity to think and feel historically, which earlier periods had in much smaller measure. It is an enormous enrichment of life, which, however, imposes upon us the responsibility not to squander this wealth thoughtlessly. The continuous effort to understand and value this possession properly belongs among the most beautiful of things life can offer to one who is not himself a creative artist. From such a concern, at least to remove obstacles from a small area, and to make the way a little bit more passable, this work has arisen; and the author repeats the request made at the outset to his colleagues, that they support him on this path with criticism and cooperation.

Bibliography

꙳ ꙳ ꙳ ꙳ ꙳ ꙳

The page numbers given in parentheses indicate the page in this book where reference to the work or author is made. The literature employed but not cited is not listed here.

Agricola, Alexander. *Musica instrumentalis deutsch*, 1528, republished 1896 by R. Eitner (p. 40)

Albert, Heinrich. *Arien, Zweiter Teil*, 1640, reprinted in DDT XII (p. 45)

Antegnati, Costanzo. *L'Arte organica*, 1608, German ed. and transl. Mainz, 1938 (p. 44)

Bach, Carl Philip Emanuel. *Versuch über die wahre Art das Clavier zu spielen*, 1753 (1759) and 1762. English transl. by W. J. Mitchell, *Essay on the True Art of Playing Keyboard Instruments*, New York, 1948 (pp. 50-51)

Beethoven, Ludwig van. *Sämtliche Briefe* (Collected Letters), Stuttgart, 1910, No. 726 (pp. 101-02)

Brahms, Johannes. Sonatas for Violin and Piano, Peters Ed. No. 3900 (pp. 28-29)

Bülow, Hans von. Prefaces and Remarks in his instructive editions of the Piano Sonatas of Beethoven, and other works (pp. 4, 11)

Cannabich, Christian. Symphony in B-flat major, in DTB XII (p. 49)

Chopin, Frédéric. Works, ed. by Karl Mikuli (p. 4)

Corelli, Arcangelo. *Concerti grossi*, Rome, 1712 (p. 42)

Couperin, François. *L'Art de toucher le Clavecin*, 1716, republished in his Complete Works, I, Paris, 1933 (pp. 17, 46-47)

Diruta, Girolamo. *Il Transilvano*, 1593, ed. in an abridged version by Karl Krebs (*Vierteljahrsschrift für Musikwissenschaft*), 1892 (p. 44)

Einstein, Alfred. *Zur deutschen Literatur für Viola da Gamba*, Leipzig, 1905 (p. 41)

Engramelle, Père. Quoted in Hans-Peter Schmitz, *Die Tontechnik des Père Engramelle*, Kassel, 1953 (p. 47)

Farina, Carlo. *Capriccio stravagante*, in Wasiliewski, *Instrumentalsätze vom Ende des XVI. bis Ende des XVII. Jahrhunderts*, Berlin, 1874. (p. 45)

Fischer, Jakob. *Erläuterungen zur Interpunktionsausgabe, Auszüge aus einer noch nicht veröffentlichten musikalischen Rhythmik und Metrik*, Vienna, 1926 (pp. 14-15)

Franck, César. Organ Works, ed. by Otto Barblan, Peters Ed. No. 3744 (p. 109)

Frescobaldi, Girolamo. *Fiori musicali*, 1635, ed. by Hermann Keller, Peters Ed. No. 4514 (pp. 44-45)

Ganassi, Silvestro. *Regola Rubertina*, 1543, *Lezione seconda*, facsimile reprint by Max Schneider, 1924 (p. 41)

Grabner, Hermann. *Allgemeine Musiklehre*, Stuttgart, 1924 (p. 55)

Grimm, Jakob, quoted in H. Gatz, *Die Musikästhetik in ihren Hauptrichtungen*, Stuttgart, 1929, p. 73 (pp. 8-9)

Grove, George. *Beethoven and His Nine Symphonies*, 1896, new ed. 1948 (p. 99)

Haas, Robert. *Aufführungspraxis der Musik*, in Bücken's *Handbuch der Musikwissenschaft*, Berlin, 1931 (pp. 31, 47-48)

Handschin, Jacques. *Der Toncharacter*, Atlantisverlag, Zurich, 1948 (p. 11)

Hanslick, Eduard. *Vom Musikalisch-Schönen*, Leipzig, 1854 (pp. 10-11)

Harich-Schneider, Eta. *Die Kunst des Cembalospiels*, Kassel, 1939 (p. 20)

Hotteterre, Jacques. *Principes de la flûte traversière . . .* 1787, German transl. by J. J. Hellwig, Kassel, 1941 (p. 40)

Keller, Hermann. *Die Orgelwerke Bachs*, Peters, 1948; *Die Klavierwerke Bachs*, Peters, 1950 (Chapters 7-9)

Krause, Christian Gottfried. *Von der musikalischen Poesie*, cited by H. Unger, in *Musikgeschichte in Selbstzeugnissen*, p. 148 (p. 31)

Krebs, Karl. Preface to the "Urtext" edition of Beethoven's Piano Sonatas, published by the Prussian Academy of the Arts, Breitkopf and Härtel, 1898, (p. 101)

Kurth, Ernst. *Grundlagen des linearen Kontrapunkts*, Bern, 1917 (pp. 4, 32)

Leblanc, Hubert. *Défense de la Basse de Viole*, 1707, German ed. by Albert Erhard, Kassel, 1951 (pp. 41-42)

Marpurg, Friedrich Wilhelm. *Die Kunst, das Clavier zu spielen*, 1750 (pp. 51-52)

Mattheson, Johann. *Das neu-eröffnete Orchestre*, 1713 (p. 55); *Kern melodischer Wissenschaft*, 1737 (pp. 18-19)

Mauthner, Fritz. *Beiträge zu einer Kritik der Sprache*, 2nd ed. (p. 13)

Mersenne, Marin. *Harmonie universelle*, Paris, 1636 (p. 41)

Moser, Andreas. *Geschichte des Violinspiels und der Violinkomposition*, 1922 (pp. 42, 46)

Muffat, Georg. Foreword to Part II of the *Florilegium musicum*, 1698, reprinted in DTÖ II (p. 42)

Musik in Geschichte und Gegenwart, Die, an encyclopedia of music, ed. by Friedrich Blume, Kassel, 1949 — (at the time of publication of the German edition of this book, this encyclopedia had reached the letter E) (p. 28)

Nottebohm, Gustav. *Beethoveniana*, I, 1872 (pp. 100-01)

Penna, Lorenzo. *Li primi albori musicali*, 1672, quoted in F. T. Arnold, *The Art of Accompaniment from a Thorough-Bass*, London, 1931 (p. 45)

Praetorius, Michael. *Syntagma musicum*, Parts II and III, 1619, facsimile ed. Kassel, 1958 (pp. 41, 43)

Quantz, Johann Joachim. *Versuch einer Anweisung die Flöte traversiere zu spielen*, 1752, facsimile ed. Kassel, 1953 (p. 40)

Raison, André. *Livre d'orgue*, 1687, reprinted by A. Guilmant, Paris, 1899 (p. 45)

Riemann, Hugo. *Musiklexikon*, 7th-11th editions; *Vademecum der Phrasierung*, 1900, 1911; *Musikalische Dynamik und Agogik*, 1884; and other writings (pp. 4, 20, 27-28, 54-57, 74)

Sancta Maria, Tomás de. *Arte de tañer fantasia . . .*, 1568, German transl. by Eta Harich-Schneider, Leipzig, 1937 (p. 44)

Scheidt, Samuel. *Tabulatura Nova*, 1624, reprinted in DDT I (p. 44); *Tabulaturbuch*, 1650 (p. 16-17)

Schenker, Heinrich. Prefaces and remarks to his edition of the Piano Sonatas of Beethoven (p. 61)

Schering, Arnold. *Geschichte der Musik in Beispielen*, Leipzig, 1931 (p. 16)

Schmitz, Hans-Peter. *Querflöte und Querflötenspiel*, Kassel, 1952 (p. 40); *Die Tontechnik des Père Engramelle*, Kassel, 1953 (p. 47)

Schütz, Heinrich. Preface to the *Becker Psalter*, 1628, new ed. Kassel (p. 17); Preface to Part II of the *Symphoniae sacrae*, 1647 (pp. 41-42)

Schweitzer, Albert. *J. S. Bach*, English transl. by Ernest Newman, Leipzig, 1911 (p. 74)

Spitta, Philipp. *J. S. Bach*, English transl., 3 vols., 1884-85, Vol. II (p. 82)

Steglich, Rudolf. Preface to the Quintets of Johann Christian Bach, in *Erbe deutscher Musik* (p. 48)

Stöhr, Richard. *Formenlehre der Musik*, Halle (pp. 54-55)

Sulzer, Johann Georg. *Allgemeine Theorie der schönen Künste*, 1771-74 (p. 19)

Türk, Daniel Gottlob. *Klavierschule*, 1789, 1802 (pp. 20, 23)

Vivaldi, Antonio. Concerto for Four Violins, reprinted in the *Bach Gesellschaft, Jahrgang* 43[1] (p. 50)

Walther, Johann Jakob. *Scherzi musicali*, 1676, reprinted in the *Erbe deutscher Musik* (p. 45)

Wiehmayer, Theodor. *Musikalische Rhythmik und Metrik*, Heinrichshofen, 1917 (pp. 28, 55, 58); *Instruktive Ausgaben klassischer Klavierwerke*, Heinrichshofen (p. 21)

Wolf, Erich, and Carl Petersen. *Das Schicksal der Musik von der Antike zur Gegenwart*, Breslau, 1923 (p. 8)

Wolf, Johannes. *Handbuch der Notationskunde*, Leipzig, I, 1913; II, 1919 (p. 4); *Geschichte der Mensuralnotation*, 1904 (p. 43)

Index

※ ※ ※ ※ ※ ※

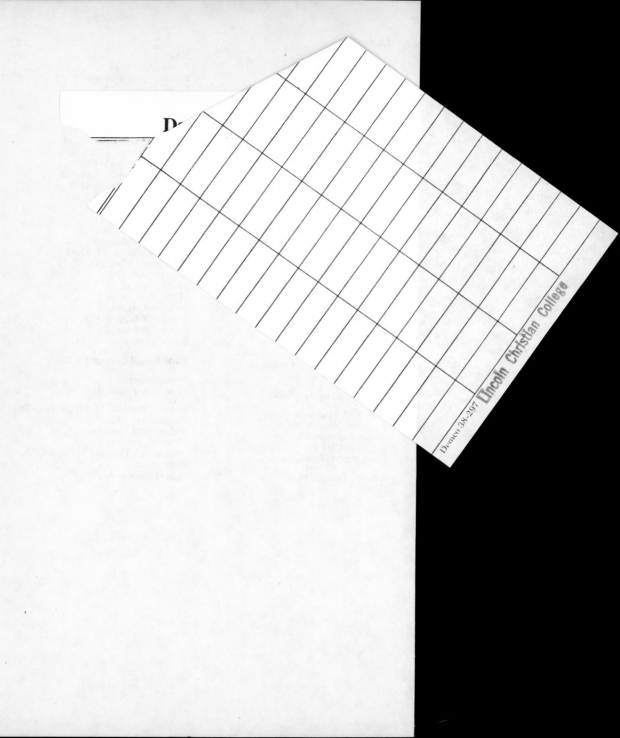